IN THIS ISSUE

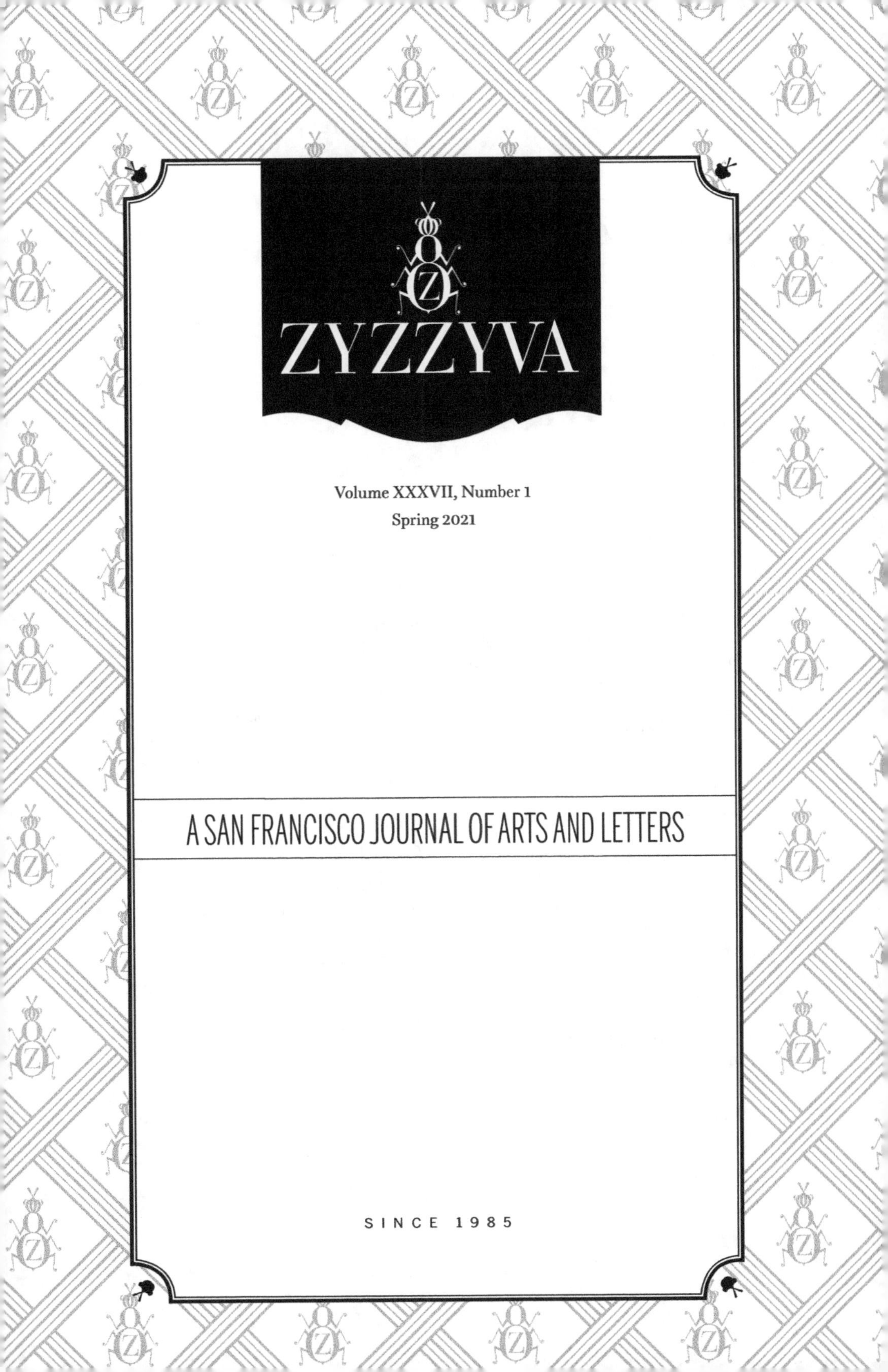

ZYZZYVA

Volume XXXVII, Number 1
Spring 2021

A SAN FRANCISCO JOURNAL OF ARTS AND LETTERS

SINCE 1985

ZYZZYVA (19604) is published in April, August, and December
by ZYZZYVA, Inc., a nonprofit, tax-exempt corporation. © 2021 ZYZZYVA, Inc.

UNDERWRITERS & PUBLISHER'S CIRCLE

Rabih Alameddine, Anonymous, In Memory of Rebecca Annitto, Henry Bowles, Lisa Brown & Daniel Handler, John Briscoe, Efrat Cogan, Paul Curtin, Carol Davis, Steven De Hart, William & Donna DeKay, In Memory of Marie Dern, Susan Diekman, Stephen Dow, Nancy & Bob Farese, In Honor of Chuck Forester, Candice Fuhrman, James Gavin, Sarah Goelet, Greer Family Foundation, James Higgins, Chuck & Sandy Hobson, Carole Holman, Jon Holman, James C. Hormel Revocable Trust, William P. Howard & Cindy Pitzer, Allan Hunter, ILO Institute, Inc., Patricia James & Joseph Di Prisco, James Jordan, Douglas Lipton, Alberta B. Lloyd, T. Dixon Long, John Luongo, John Marx, Nion McEvoy & Leslie Berriman, Dawn McGuire, Asena McKeown, Robert Meave, Myriam & Richard Misrach, Chris Mittelstaedt, Gail Moore, Gale & Rich Morrison, Jeffrey Moskowitz, Alden Mudge, Dennis Murray, Steve & Nancy Oliver, Constance Peabody, Susan Pritzker, Arthur Reidel, Jamie Rosenthal Wolf & David Wolf via the Rosenthal Family Foundation, Gregory Sarris, Steven Sattler, Alice Sebold, Kevin Smokler, Frances Stroh, Carolyn & Eric Svenson, Chris Svenson, Lisa Taylor, TooFar Media, Jack M. & Rose Ullman Foundation, Julia Wackenheim & Scott Gimple, Peter Walker, Peter Booth Wiley, Barbara & Charlie Winton

PATRONS

Anonymous, Laurel Beeler, Will & Ashley Bunnett, Peter Brantley, Nancy Calef & Jody Weiner, Nora Camagna, Marie Ciepiela, Barnaby Conrad III, Maureen Cronin, Bill Curtsinger, Marie Dern, Frances Dinkelspiel, Glenn D'Mello, Maureen Fan, Dale Freeman, Blair Fuller, Leah & Jerry Garchik, John L. Geiger, Philip Gelston, Lyn Grant, Jennifer Grimes, Walt Halland, Lynda Heidemann, James P. Higgins, James Hormel, Franck Ilmain, Charles & Naomie Kremer, Michael Krouse, Michelle Latiolais, Joy Leo, Anthony Ley, Diane Liguori, Maxwell James Magid, Lou Mathews, Anthony Mohr, Douglas Ravas, Art Reidel, Bryant G. Rice, Jason Roberts, Roy Ruderman & Kirsten Schlenger, Patricia Unterman & Tim Savinar, Motoyuki Shibata, Moira Shourie, C.J. Singh, Roger Sippl, Len & Jan Smith, Bruce Snider & Lysley Tenorio, Stephen Thompson, Bonnie Stuppin, Richard Walter, Ted Weinstein, Jerry Weissman, Pattie Wells, Meredith White, Peter Wiley, Rolf Yngve, Janis M. Zivic

MEMBERS

Irene Adler, Lisa Alvarez & Andrew Tonkovich, Michele Anderson, Anonymous, Stewart Applin, Andy Armendariz, Paul Beatty, Laurel Beeler, Judy Bernhard & Byron Spooner, Richard Bohannon, Tecoah & Tom Bruce, Jack Calvert, David Cattin, Marie Ciepiela, Carmela Ciuraru, Denis Clifford, Brian Cook, Jen Craft, Drew Cushing, Jeffrey Davis, Joe Donnelly, John Engell, Megan Feist, Daniel Feldman, Janet A. Fiorenza, Ford & Goldsmith, Rebecca Foust, Marilyn Friedman, Lisa Gallien, Ann Gateley, Dagoberto Gilb, David Lance Goines, Glen David Gold, Robert & Sarah Goldsmith, Stephen Gomez, Judith Gordon, Teresa & Andrew Gunther, Mary Guterson, Melissa Halabe, Diana Hardy, Richard Harrah, Therese Harris, Robert Hass & Brenda Hillman, David Hecht, David Hernandez, Kathleen Hudson, Franck Ilmain, Brett Hall Jones, Jane Kahn & Michael Bien, Kenneth Kottka, Chaney Kwak, Robert & Mary Ladd, Michael Larsen & Elizabeth Pomada, Dorianne Laux, Ashley Nelson Levy, Tara MacMahon, Dino Nartea Makabenta, Roberto Manduchi, Matthew Markovich, Pamela Martin, Toni Martin, Robert McEntegart, Anthony Mohr, Jen Craft & Howard Moorin, Gale & Rich Morrison, Charles Mosher, Meryl Natchez, Alex Niculescu, Dan O'Brien, Lori Ostlund & Anne Raeff, Bridget Quinn, Colleen Regan, David Rhymer, Bryant Rice, Nicki Richesin, Jennifer Richter, Alan Rinzler, Charles Rodewald, Luis Romero, Seth Rosenfeld & Heidi Benson, Jim Ruland, Charles F. Rund, Dan Saccani, Marcia Schneider, Ronald Schoenmehl (in honor of Rebecca Thomas), Barbara Seymour, Elizabeth Sibson-Tuan & Bertrand Tuan, Julia Flynn Siler, Kevin Smokler, Nat Sobel, Octavio Solis, Doug Straus, Bonnie Stuppin, DS Sulaitis, Elizabeth Tallent, Tess Taylor, Matthew VanFossen, Michael Ward, Pam Weiss, Cynthia White, Stanley Zumbiel

SPECIAL THANKS

ZYZZYVA is grateful for support from the National Endowment for the Arts, The Literary Arts Emergency Fund, and Thomas R. Burke. Visual Art Fund established by Kevin Smokler.

CONTENTS

FRONT & BACK COVERS

Dave McClinton, *Fortitude IV,* 2020, digital collage, courtesy: the artist

Dave McClinton, *Tired II,* 2017, digital collage, courtesy: the artist

Zyzzyva.

(ZIZ-zi-va) n. A San Francisco
literary journal; any of various
tropical American weevils of the
genus *Zyzzyva.* The last word in
the Oxford English Dictionary.

FORTHCOMING

No. 121 publishes in August 2021.

**Apply for the Fall 2021
Online Certificate Program in Novel Writing**

ACCEPTING APPLICATIONS APRIL 12 THROUGH JUNE 4

Learn More: continuingstudies.stanford.edu

GLEN BAXTER

Social distancing had finally allowed Uncle Frank..., 2020, ink and crayon on paper, 15 x 11 inches

VODKA
CERTIFIED ORGANIC
SMALL BATCH-LIMITED RELEASE
4X DISTILLED-80 PROOF-ALC 40% BY VOL
HUMBOLDT DISTILLERY
USDA ORGANIC
TM

LETTER FROM THE EDITOR

Dear Readers,

At the beginning of George Dyson's latest book, *Analogia*, he describes how, in 1716, Gottfried Wilhelm Leibniz hoped his *calculus ratiocinator* (an instrument that brilliantly anticipated digital computing) would "work out, by an infallible calculus, the doctrines most useful for life." With this device, Leibniz imagined, "The human race will have a new kind of instrument which will increase the power of the mind much more than optical lenses strengthen the eyes."

I am struck by the analogy and how well it lends itself to piercing Leibniz's optimism; for just as vision is not, in itself, perception, information (or data) is not knowledge.

Certainly, we know that now. As we mark over a year into the COVID-19 pandemic and more than 500,000 Americans dead from the disease, it's hard to imagine a more stark or poignant demonstration of the bifurcation technology has wrought in twenty-first-century life: astonishing advances and, simultaneously, devastating damage.

We marvel at how swiftly multiple vaccines have been developed, but despair at the lethal silos of misinformation that have gripped so many.

Human ingenuity for molding our environs is incomparable in the natural world. But we're too often blind to what we're actually creating. Computing technology is not the first means by which humanity has imagined and then built a system that we later feel trapped within: we've done this with religious and economic systems, too.

Perhaps the defining distinction of our current predicament is that we're immersed in media bent on increasing engagement, where algorithms tailor a narrative to each of us. Like others, I often wonder how long or how well democracies can function upon a rapidly eroding foundation of shared reality.

Could Leibniz have imagined that exponentially more powerful computing instruments than the one he'd devised would undermine our ability to reach consensus on the basic facts of what *is*, let alone how best to deal with those facts?

The work gathered here reflects how ill at ease we are within our own constructions, but also reminds us of the essential synergy between art and science—how important literature is, as a critical challenge to technology's momentum, as a creative force driving innovation, and, sometimes, as a conscience. Literature brings both historical context and imagination to the conversation. Without these, our vision, however sharp, lacks perspective, lacks essential information. Without these, increasing the "power of the mind" may lead to madness.

Here in San Francisco, the term "tech" is pervasive, and together with a cloud of associations, seems to have overshadowed its roots. Let's not reduce "technology" to "tech." Let's revive the presence of both *techne* (art, craft, skill) and *logos* (the word) in our engagement with technology.

Our relationship to it shouldn't be reduced to either constant anxiety or weary resignation to a world of relentless growth hacking.

True technological innovation still occurs—it is more than social media and delivery apps—and it remains an extraordinary expression of human ingenuity. But innovations could also be increasingly risky gambits, in that we are creating systems we may ultimately be unable to control. With all that is at stake, we must keep a poetic, philosophical, and literary gaze on such enormous power and potential.

Yours,

L.

MY ONE AND ONLY VERY INCREDIBLE AMAZING LOVE

LEE CONELL

Fifty-four likes. In the photo: Courtney and me, squished beneath a fleece blanket in front of the television. I've just broken up with Jake in L.A. and moved back to Nashville, where Courtney and I grew up. We were once best friends. Then off to separate colleges—Courtney stayed in Nashville to study biochemistry, I headed to California to study film. Our interactions became limited to texts on Monday nights (when we watched the same bad reality TV show) plus a couple of lunches when I came home during winter breaks. Growing apart felt a little tragic but mostly developmentally normal.

But my return to Tennessee combined with my heartbroken state has made Courtney behave tonight like we never grew apart at all, like we're best friends again, like we're not twenty-five but eighteen. Tonight, we watch bad reality TV together. Tonight, we share snacks from the Piggly Wiggly. Tonight, Courtney grins big at my dumbest jokes. There's something in her kindness to me that feels like an act of charity, which is maybe the same thing as an act of dominance.

The blanket we're beneath is covered in squiggly orange lines and zigzagging turquoise chevrons, what Courtney calls "Aztec Boho." It's displayed prominently in the photo she posts of us. Months later, user otterthink20 will comment, *That blanket is appropriative and is* NOT *ahistorical and given the real platform you have Courtney you should maybe think twice.* But in the moment the photo is taken, Courtney has no platform. She's focused only on the way the blanket's bright colors add visual intrigue to what would otherwise be a boring image of two women watching television on a Monday night.

Courtney's been in the lab twelve hours purifying proteins; she's exhausted, but she still looks so much more beautiful than me. Under the TV's light, her blond hair glows like a cloud radiant with iceblink. After my shift at Pizza of Yr Dreams, my greasy dark hair looks like an oil spill. But I don't need to wash my hair for Courtney, especially since we're just marathoning *My One and Only Very Incredible Amazing Love,* or #MooVial as it's called online—the show where a group of women compete for a proposal from a man who must say, before getting down on one knee, "You *are* my one and only very incredible amazing love." Courtney and I have been laughing at the desperate women on the show all evening, but as soon as Courtney lifts up her phone to photograph us, we stop smiling and look serious. That's because if we *were* to smile, it would seem we were advertising our friendship like it was a soup or a fizzy water for sale. Our goal is to advertise that our friendship is beyond easy advertisement, is authentic. Of course, I guess just by saying such a thing I'm undermining our authenticity, which I don't mean to do. I just don't know how else to talk about it: Courtney and I are definitely selling something about our friendship in this moment, but that act of selling isn't duplicitous or corporate. It simply seems to add to the earnestness and the value of the moment.

After she posts the photo, I read the caption. *That's right everyone, history is never history… The Emo Jewess and the Dumb Blonde have been reunited!*

My screenname in high school was EmoJewess14. Courtney's was DumbBlondeTN23. At age fourteen, we'd discovered that if you mocked

16 yourself, others couldn't mock you in the same way. Courtney was Barbie-doll gorgeous, but she also was incredibly shy, wouldn't raise her hands in class, and her dad lived in a trailer. All this made the other kids in school want to call her stupid, even though (or because of) the way she smoked them in math and science. I was a target for different reasons: I was one of the few Jewish kids in the school, plus I wore all black, which made jackass Todd shout at me, in front of his friends, that I should start an emo band called The Angsty Christ Killers. His friends laughed and I laughed loudest of all, to seem like I was in on it. That night, my new screenname was born. (Secretly, I longed to know who the other 13 EmoJewesses were.)

"Are you going to like the post?" Courtney asks, after the picture of us has been up for a few minutes.

I like the post. But seeing our childhood internet nicknames resurrected on social media unnerves me. "Maybe I should write about my old internet self," I say to Courtney. "Writing's not like making a film. It's free."

But she hasn't heard me. *My One and Only* is back and the women go on a cruise to continue to try to win the heart of Bryan, a realtor who tells the camera he's truly on the show for love, not fame. "I'm here because I wanted kids, like, yesterday," Bryan says. We watch the women competing to be the most beautiful in the least intimidating, most approachable America's Sweetheartiest ways. Their age and jobs parade beneath their face on screen. Nanny, 24. Dental Hygienist, 26. Makeup Artist, 25. During the commercial break, we look up the women online. The favorites on the show have already quit their day jobs and are paid by companies for sponsored posts on social media. They're sent teeth whitener, or sunglasses, or jellybeans meant to make hair glossier. They push the products in one photo, and then in the next, they take a selfie with their dog. "Is she selling that dog, too?" I ask

Courtney, leaning over her shoulder.

"No, she just actually loves the dog, I think." Then Courtney looks right at me. "I don't want to go to work tomorrow," she says, like she's confessing a sin.

I want to tell Courtney that in my opinion she doesn't exactly *"go to work"* like normal people. She's in school. She's getting her PhD in biochemistry while I serve pizza and live with my parents. But like I said, we've grown apart since college, and such honesty seems not only too cruel, but too intimate. I look away from Courtney and dip my hand into a wimpled bag of chips.

Twenty-nine likes. A photo of a yellow "DEAD END" sign. It's been a month since I've watched #MooVial with Courtney, and we haven't seen each other in all that time. We message each other things like, *So busy, let's get together soon?* Courtney hasn't posted in weeks, and now, suddenly, this "DEAD END." I can tell from two magnolia trees just behind the sign that she's taken the photo near where Courtney's mom and stepdad live. Her mom's okay now, but she was depressed for a while, in the won't-go-outside way, and Courtney went to college and grad school nearby in part to keep an eye on her. Courtney's caption reads: *Saw this on my walk today… Could be a warning for cars but lately feels like a warning for women in science PhD programs.* A few hours later, she deletes the post.

Something in me cracks open when I see the post is gone. I open my email. I write Courtney a letter, telling her that though I don't really post on social media now because it gives me anxiety, I still pay attention to *her* posts, and the dead-end sign post resonated, and does she remember I once wanted to direct films? Talk about your dead ends: I'm poor, I have no connections, and I'm a woman. I tell her that now, on my breaks from the pizza shop, I'm trying to compose innovative nonfiction essays in which I write smartly analytical descriptions of

18 my old social media posts from high school/college, and I got the idea from her, from when she used our high school screen names the other day, does she remember?

Except once I've written all that down, I feel a wave of embarrassment. Everything I said sounds, for lack of a more sophisticated word, emo. And I'm better than the screen name from my youth. I have to be. I delete my email draft.

Ninety-three likes. A week or so after "DEAD END." Courtney and me in Centennial Park, our middle fingers raised at a line of tourists. I'm glum that day because it would have been my two-year anniversary with Jake. The park, Courtney believes, will cheer me up. It's full of dogs and ducks, and also houses Nashville's fake Parthenon—a full-scale replica of the Parthenon in Greece. We take pictures in front of the replica's columns, pretending we aren't both in debt, pretending we're not near a Starbucks and Rite Aid, pretending we're on a real vacation. It's funny to feel like tourists in the city where we grew up. Courtney says, as we take our photos, "I really thought I'd have lived a lot more places by this point."

"We should get out of here," I say. "I can't live with my parents much longer. Let's go to Paris or something."

Courtney suggests going to Starbucks first. We each get a hot tea, which we're pretty sure offers free refills as long as we reuse our teabags. When we sit down at a table inside, I ask, "What was the 'dead end' post about?"

Courtney looks into her paper cup. "One of my professors just skeeves me out." The word "skeeves" makes me think of "sleeves," makes me think of some man in a big woolen sweater embracing Courtney from behind, and I think of the blanket we huddled under to watch *My One and Only,* how warm that was.

"What happened?" I ask.

She responds too quickly. "He thinks I'm some dumb blonde."

"Did he do something?"

"I'm going to post the one of us flipping off the tourists. Is that okay?"

"Yeah," I say.

"I don't have to. I know you think you're too good for social media."

I scratch my neck.

"I'm just kidding," Courtney says. "You're not much of a snob."

A group of high school girls across from us start laughing. They sound like they love each other so much. I somehow choose this moment to tell Courtney that I'm thinking about writing these micro-essays in which I describe the photos I posted on social media in college. "I'll be detailing the pictures," I say, "but also everything outside the frame."

"Hmm," Courtney says.

I grip my paper cup like there's no tea in it, like I'm begging for change. "What's wrong with that?"

"It's just that I've heard you should never include social media in your art. It dates it."

I try to loosen my grip on my cup.

"I mean shouldn't you be aiming for the timeless? I just think you *could* create something timeless and amazing, if you trusted yourself as an artist."

I say, calm as I can, "I'll take it into consideration."

"I can tell you won't. You think I'm an idiot." Then she starts to cry.

Obviously, I apologize immediately. "You're *not* an idiot." I grab her arm. "You're so much smarter than me. You're getting your PhD and I'm just trying to write stupid micro things and I haven't actually gotten one word down yet, okay?"

"This isn't about you." She pushes my hands away. "I just need to be alone. Will you leave me the hell alone?"

Seventy-nine likes. Three weeks later. A photo of Courtney in a floppy hat. The closed-lip smile she does when she thinks she should be grinning but is self-conscious about her teeth. *On a grand adventure. My account will be deactivated for a few weeks but can't wait to see your faces again soon, my loves!*

When I see her post at work, surrounded by bubbling cheese and burning crust, I tremble. Let me be clear: I'm pretty sure I was never in love with Courtney, except in that intense way you're in love with anybody good-looking who's unexpectedly nice to you in adolescence. But still, this announced absence catches me off balance. She's left without a word to me.

I step outside the pizza shop, hunch over a picnic table, and open the notes on my phone. I try to start an essay about a profile picture from my freshman year of college, me in all black holding up the cat that belonged to the boy who took my virginity. At the top of the note, I write the title: "Freudian Much?" I can't come up with anything else.

I close out of notes. I text one of our mutual friends asking if she's heard from Courtney. *C dropped out of her PhD and went on that show,* Allison says. *You know My One and Only Blah Blah? Have you heard of it?*

No, I respond. *I don't watch that sexist shit.*

One thousand and five hundred and thirty-two likes. Courtney in a metallic mini-wrap dress, her hips canted, her smile open. She's pointing to her hair, which is gathered in what looks to me like a gorgeous chignon. *Screenshot from tonight's episode of #MooVial … What does my messy topknot have to do with my journey to find love? Find out tonight …*

It's been about a month since filming wrapped. Courtney's returned to Nashville, but I haven't seen her yet. I texted her weeks ago and told her I knew she was on the show and what happened? She told me she's signed a nondisclosure agreement but added, *It's wild babe how quickly life can change.* I didn't respond. But I read spoilers online: Courtney's won the show. She's engaged.

Allison invites me to a watch party, but I watch the premiere alone in my room while my parents watch a documentary about chimpanzees. The show has an introductory video for Logan, a thick-necked fitness coach looking for his soulmate, followed by intro videos for the women who will be major competitors for his heart this season. The women share their names and then either a traumatic life story or a bad joke. A short skinny woman with almost no eyebrows speaks about losing her mother in a car accident. A tall skinny woman with bowed lips speaks about her brother in jail. A woman with eyelashes like weapons says, "Logan, I'm not just a karate master, I'm a Ninja Love Princess, and I'm coming for you, hiiiiyahh!"

Then, there she is, on a park bench in a lab coat, holding a beaker. She looks up, lips parting. "Oh, hi," she says, "I'm Courtney and I'm a Professional Dumb Blonde. I mean, I dropped out of my biochemistry PhD program to find love. What could be dumber, right? At least that's what my friends say, but I can't wait to prove them wrong." She tosses the beaker over her shoulder. "One of my favorite dumb blonde jokes is: Why'd the blonde get fired from the M&M factory?" She smiles so sweetly. "She kept throwing out all the Ws."

After this intro, the show lists Courtney's occupation as Ex-PhD/ Professional Dumb Blonde whenever she appears onscreen. When she meets Logan with the other women, she takes him aside on the yacht and tells him a sad story about her dad losing his factory job to technology and being an alcoholic in his trailer. Logan tries to one-up her with a sad story about his own dad being an alcoholic in his mansion. But just like rock always beats scissors, trailer is always sadder than mansion. Courtney wins in the dad trauma department and Logan's duly impressed. "I'm really myself around Courtney," he tells the camera. At the end of the episode, Courtney advances to the next round.

Even though we haven't talked much since she told me to leave her alone, Courtney calls me after the first show airs. She's upset because she watched with a few friends from college, all of them with majors in what Courtney calls "the fanatically sincere areas," and they were scandalized by the Dumb Blonde nickname. The college friends said the producers were demeaning her. Courtney told the college friends it was only a joke. The college friends said Courtney was being objectified. Courtney told the college friends that she felt objectified by their cynicism, their judgment, and that the producers hadn't manipulated her.

"So why are you calling *me* about this?" I ask.

"Because you know the nickname's history. We were reclaiming what was offensive. That's what Candice and Joelle don't get. The producers are referencing *my* joke. Like if they called you 'Emo Jewess' for example—"

"It's not the same," I say. "Dumb Blonde is less ethnically specific than 'Jewess.' You act like those nicknames were equally demeaning, when historically it's more complicated."

"Would it be fairer to you if I called myself Dumb Blonde Trailer Trash?"

I take a breath. Courtney hangs up. Later that day she posts a screenshot from the show. Courtney and Logan dancing together during a special private concert with some band I've never heard of. The band singing about America and love and prairies. Courtney's grinning. With teeth. My mom's voice floats through my bedroom door. She wants to know why I left my hair in the shower drain again. What motivates me, she wants to know, to do such a thing at my current adult age?

I open my notebook. I'm trying now to write about this profile photo of me in front of a McDonald's at nineteen, performatively scowling in a way I think makes me look older. "An Unhappy Meal," I title it. But I can't think up what else to write.

One trillion likes (basically). My birthday. Courtney with three women from #*MooVial*, surrounded by mountains. They all look like people who might have "dance like no one's watching" tattooed on their inner wrists. They smile like they've been friends forever. They wear tight flannel shirts and leggings.

A few days after, Courtney calls and wishes me a happy belated birthday. She says she's sorry about snapping at me the last time we talked, and I say, "Don't worry." She invites me over to watch the new episode of *My One and Only* with her tomorrow. Another contestant is going to watch it with us, too, if that's okay. "That's fine," I lie. The contestant is the short woman with no eyebrows who was kicked off the show a week ago. Logan said, "I just didn't see a lifelong relationship with Lauren G." I'm prepared to hate Lauren G., who was a little cruel on the show, but in person it turns out she's nice and smells like lilacs. Lauren G. says, "Courtney calls you her brilliant lodestar."

When the show starts, Lauren G. and Courtney cuddle beneath the Aztec Boho blanket. I sit in the adjacent armchair. On the episode, Courtney and Logan go on what Logan calls "a pivotal date." "Is this the helicopter one?" Lauren G. asks. "Right before the Eiffel Tower date, right?"

Courtney, blushing, nods.

Inside the helicopter, over a bottle of champagne, TV-Courtney opens up to Logan about her last relationship. "I loved him," she says, "and it was really hard to put it all out there and leave with nothing. He wasn't ready to commit."

Logan's blue eyes go soft. "But listen, Court? If this is going to work, I need you to let down your walls."

A tear runs down her face. "I'm trying, Logan."

"Court, I need you to *more than try*."

"Total bullshit," I say to the non-TV Courtney.

24

Courtney frowns. Lauren G. narrows her eyes.

"Bret was ready to commit," I say. "You told me you just found him boring."

"I wasn't referencing Bret here. I was talking about Jordan."

"Jordan? The rebound?"

"Jordan was important to me."

"No, he wasn't. I remember."

Courtney and Lauren G. exchange looks. Then Courtney smiles with her mouth closed. I suddenly feel the weight of my weightlessness in her life. Not only had I not known she was dropping out of her PhD program, I can barely recall her talking about Jordan at all. Still, what right does Lauren G. have to *exchange looks* with Courtney about me?

I drink two glasses of wine, quickly, and spend the rest of the episode making fun of Logan's hair, questioning his intelligence, until Courtney says, "I know you've read the spoilers."

"So?"

"I'm engaged to Logan."

"In the fake TV way."

"My feelings are real."

"I'm getting more salsa for these chips," I announce.

When I'm in the kitchen, Courtney corners me. This has never occurred between us before, really: A confrontation, the kind that happens all the time on *My One and Only*, the kind Courtney has suddenly become very skilled at. She wants to know what my problem is. She's sick of how I look down on her.

"I don't look down on *you*." I take her hand. "We *always* made fun of the show."

"But now it's not a show to me. There's so much footage you don't even see. Logan can be really thoughtful."

"I'm sure he's nice. I'm sure he also seems too stupid to be threatening to your self-worth and that's the only reason he's even a thing to you."

"Please don't psychoanalyze me." She grabs another bag of chips from the top of the fridge and pulls it open so hard, it nearly rips down the middle. "Don't do the Sensitive Smart Girl thing. It's an act."

"Like you calling yourself a Dumb Blonde?"

"That isn't an act. It's a *joke*."

I tell her no, it isn't a joke, it's a branding strategy to get airtime on the show. To seem simultaneously outrageous and harmless. She says nothing. "What's this whole *One and Only* thing really about?" I ask. "What happened with that professor?"

Courtney swallows. Then she flips me off, just like we flipped off those tourists. Without another word, she goes back to the living room. I leave.

Three trillion likes. The proposal photo. The sun an orange ball over the ocean. Logan, down on one knee. Courtney, wearing a red gown and grinning (teeth showing) while crying. After the proposal, Courtney tells the camera, "I guess you could say the Dumb Blonde finally got smart about love!" It's clear a producer asked her, "Did the Dumb Blonde get smart about love?" and encouraged her to use those words in answering, and it's also clear that Courtney doesn't care, will say whatever she needs to say to get the producer out of her face so she can be alone with Logan, without cameras. She's luminous.

A few days later, a tabloid reaches out to me about Courtney. They offer to pay me so much money for dirt on her. The pizza place is barely paying enough for me to keep up with my loan payments. Of course, I don't have a lot of dirt, but I could direct them to that professor. I still don't know what happened, but there's clearly a story. And I realize just like that: I don't want to write about my own social media. I want to write Courtney's story. Maybe I could actually sell that to some magazine, and on my own terms.

 I text Courtney asking if we can talk. She says she's busy, but I can come over for a little bit the next morning. She has a new couch in her apartment, something sleeker, and the Aztec Boho blanket is gone. It's the first time we've seen each other since she flipped me off.

She makes me a cup of coffee from some brand called EarthGod that will pay her lots of money if she'll post about their sustainably harvested beans. I ask her if she's planning to leave Nashville and move to California with Logan. "We're taking it step by step," Courtney says, "but that's the idea. What are you here for, anyway?"

"Me?"

"What do you want?"

So I tell her about the tabloid reaching out and that I want to write an inventive essay in the form of descriptions of her posted photos instead of my own and she shouldn't be self-conscious or anything, but this essay will operate off of a sort of docu-fictional aesthetic, is an examination of the contemporary intersection between love and narcissism, of how the most intimate experiences (romantic love/female friendship) are becoming in themselves public branding phenomena, and I do want to get the essay out soon, if possible, because the form itself will quickly begin to seem dated as social media platforms change shape in ways I can't yet predict, plus Courtney will only be relevant in the media for so long, and I'm not exactly asking permission or anything, but I do want to make sure Courtney is informed about where I'm at, artistically.

Courtney interlaces her fingers around the coffee cup.

"Are you mad?" I ask.

"Am I mad?" She smiles at me. Close-mouthed. Then she says my essay itself is a kind of branding, and won't I be using it to increase my own followers, in turn increasing people's interest in my art? I can act all pure-of-heart but my very stance of purity is of course part of my own brand, and she's given me a pass for *months* because she's pretty sure Jake was emotionally abusive, but she's done cutting me so much slack, and she truly loves Logan and her new friends from the show, and she also misses her science, more than anything, but I don't know what it was like, I never *really* asked what the work environment was like for her, plus at least her new reality-TV-star brand is being used for good, to pay off student loans *and* to help fund a gym for lower-income kids that Logan wants to start, whereas my brand will always be pathetic, a Sad Pure White She-Artist brand, which is boring, which has been done for centuries or at least decades, which is the most hypocritical brand of all, in her opinion, and I'm clearly prepared to use her like everyone else, taking our friendship and exploiting it for my own ambitions, only I'm more annoying because I pretend like I'm *doing something artistic,* and haven't I noticed what kind of friend I've become, when's the last time I asked her questions about her life, about how she's coping with all these changes, an engagement and a weird sort of fame and the end of her scientific career because of this professor, and yet *she's* somehow the narcissist because of her increased use of social media, and she's tired of pretending like the history of our friendship is some sweet sterling thing, when it's been clear to her for ages that I always treated her as stupid, saw her as merely beautiful, someone who conferred a gleam to my own outsider status in school, which yeah, had a little to do with my being Jewish and with historical intolerance or whatever, but had a lot more to do with my being awkward and needy, don't I even know that, a grown-ass woman, and maybe she'll go back to science but maybe it's also okay for her to take time to be in love, to heal, and no, *now* she doesn't want to talk about what went wrong in our friendship, she doesn't want to give me more material, she wants me out of her apartment/life, and she never wants to see my Sad Pure White She-Artist face again, *out out out.*

So, I leave.

 So, I get in my car.

Okay. She isn't being entirely unfair. But if I'm really concerned about my brand, would I put what she said about me in this essay? Would I make room for doubts about my motivations? Would I allow myself to seem so manipulative?

Or am I writing out our final conversation because, conversely, being upfront about what she said somehow makes it less true, less powerful, less valid? And is that itself manipulative? Is it a form of denial, of self-excusal?

Everything I write, suddenly, seems like the opposite of micro. Seems like part of a bigger story with ambitions I can't completely grasp and limitations I haven't tried hard enough to see.

Two trillion likes. Logan and Courtney in front of the Parthenon. They've got their arms around each other and they're grinning. There's no product being pushed. And although he's in the photo, there's no mention of Logan in Courtney's caption. Instead: *Learned so much today thanks to a private tour of the Parthenon! Did you know the original replica of the Parthenon was built in 1897 for the Tennessee Centennial Exposition? It wasn't designed to last longer than the Centennial but when it came time to tear it down, Nashvillians cried and wept because it had become an icon. They wouldn't let the replica be torn down. Eventually the replica was falling apart but so beloved that the whole thing was rebuilt in more durable concrete. So in a way it lasted but in another way it's totally fake. I think that's really cool. What are the important historical monuments in your city/town?? #knowyourcity #loveyourcity #knowyourhistory*

I'm on a break at work when I see this photo. My lungs start to hurt. Nearby, a pizza crust is burning. I want to write something in the comment box. If I can only craft the perfect witty response, maybe that will give me permission to re-enter Courtney's life. But nothing I've got to say in response seems like what it needs to be. Nothing I think up seems incredible or amazing or right or close to what I really want to express. Nothing seems like love. ✄

Lee Conell is the author of the novel The Party Upstairs *(Penguin Press), winner of the Wallant Award, and the story collection* Subcortical *(Johns Hopkins University Press), winner of a Story Prize Spotlight Award.*

WALDEN TWO

BENJAMIN VOIGT

In room 210, you invented the Internet:
with glass eyes and a skeletal beard,

you daisy-chained beige towers into fire-hazards,
and we were your lab rats

answering questions about positive and negative
externalities.

True or false: language is all there is,
and there is no such thing

as thought, only private behavior, dinner bells
we ring ourselves,

both the doctors and the dogs.
I've held onto that last line for a long time,

and don't know if I've used it right,
or if this is a glitch

in my programming I'm still debugging.
Imagine me after school

turning it in my head while you're talking about
doorknobs again,

Wittgenstein's hobby,
with Jesse, the goth kid with the lip ring

who insisted I didn't understand the Tractatus
because I didn't.

I still don't,
and I don't know why I'm building this maze

for you to run through,
when I could just come out and say it:

I want to hold you
like the sweater at the consignment shop

my mother saw you try on
years after I'd left town with such fervor

she believed
you'd never belonged to anything or anyone.

I want to hold you
like Skinner did his kid when he lifted her

from his box, a perfect place to grow up
if you believe

we're not much different than robots,
which we always joked

you were: an advanced model teacher
who just shut off

upright in the corner after everyone left.
Now I see online

you've got a child of your own, and I wonder
what her name is,

32

because I was yours
until I caught something hiding

behind my eyes, a minotaur
at my center I didn't want to tame or slay.

Let's say it's Rose,
because, even by any other, she will be

what her conditions condition her to be
and won't, the duck or rabbit

slipping through the underbrush at dusk,
whatever you were,

and whatever you forget you were
to make it through the woods.

Benjamin Voigt is a poet and critic who teaches about technology and poetry at Macalester College in Minnesota.

THE FIXERS

TROY JOLLIMORE

Joel and Ethan Coen's 1996 film, *Fargo,* begins with the following statement:

"This is a true story. The events depicted in this film took place in Minnesota in 1987. At the request of the survivors, the names have been changed. Out of respect for the dead, the rest has been told exactly as it occurred."

The statement was, of course, false. So far as we know, there was no desperate man, in Minnesota or anywhere in the Midwest, who hired two goons to kidnap his wife in the hopes of stealing the ransom money that would be paid by his wealthy father-in-law, only to see his rather poorly laid plans go predictably and tragically astray. A bald-faced lie, then? Or just a falsehood? Really, was it even that? Are words shown at the beginning of a film being *asserted,* or are they simply *there?* It is human nature to believe something when it is told to you by another human being. Though in this case no human being was speaking. There were just words, disembodied words, appearing as part of an experience produced by a technological artifact.

These words, not spoken by anyone, don't even add anything to the story. They alter our understanding of the story, informing us, albeit

34 falsely, that this is not merely a story, but something that actually took place, something real human beings actually lived through. They tell us the genre of the work and its relation to life; they tell us that what we are about to witness is no idle fantasy but is based in fact. Someone had to suffer these horrific events. People ended up dead because of them. So any implausibility in the ensuing plot would have to be taken in and considered against the background assumption that this is a piece of history, of the real world. *This actually happened. This is the kind of thing that actually happens.*

TOLD EXACTLY AS IT OCCURRED

We don't want the audience to know it's a film.

—Film editor Harold Kress[1]

There are technologies for the hands, and technologies for the eyes. There are technologies whose direct effect is to allow us to manipulate reality, and there are technologies whose primary purpose is to communicate, to provide representations of reality. Of course, things cannot really be divided up so neatly. New visions enable new manipulations, new manipulations lead to new visions. The very idea of using technology to manipulate reality only arises once language, which is itself a technology, is fully in place.

Representational technologies do not merely depict reality in a neutral way, capturing what was already there in a symbolic pattern. They alter. They distort. They give birth to. The original matter must be modified to fit the scheme. It must be transformed into "content." Representational technologies necessitate emphasizing some elements

---

1 In Oldham, Gabriella. *First Cut: Conversations with Film Editors* (University of California Press, 1992), p. 96.

of the matter at the expense of others (or, more radically, the technology performs that task itself). The person with a camera gets to decide—is forced to decide—where the camera is pointed. The editor gets to decide—is forced to decide—what gets cut and what gets displayed. What is silenced and what is made available. What will be made visible and what will become, or remain, invisible.

Because technologies enable new depictions of reality, they enable new ways of forming and promulgating falsehoods. The history of technology may be thought of as the history of the invention of new ways for us to be fooled, to be deceived, to be duped. Each new generation of innovators invents new forms of wool to be pulled over our eyes. The invention of the camera, for instance, opened up new possibilities for deception and thus changed the nature of lying. Maybe it changed the nature of truth, too.

The same can be said of the invention of storytelling, which of course radically predates the invention of the camera. Stories are technologies. A story is a way of saying something about human life, and in creating one, or passing one on, or hearing and believing one, we change our understanding of human life and in so doing change what human life is. The implicit message behind every story is *This is something that happened to someone. This is the kind of thing that happens.* And thus: *This is the kind of thing that could happen to you.*

NEVER HEARD OF HIM, DON'T VOUCH FOR HIM

EDDIE MANNIX: *What kind of name is Thora, anyway?*
THORA THACKER: *It's a name that nineteen million readers trust.*
—Hail, Caesar!

Let me tell you about something that happened to me. Now there is the beginning to a story we can trust. Or at least, we can trust the story

36 so far as we can trust the speaker. The earliest stories were probably first personal, accounts of the teller's actions and experiences. Prior to the invention of recording technology, the half-life of stories was presumably quite short; a story could travel only so far before degrading beyond all usefulness, beyond belief. A story told by a person who had not themselves lived it, or who did not hear it from the person who had themselves lived it, would be less likely to be taken as a literal, let alone a reliable report.

In *Fargo*, when Jerry Lundegaard, the pathetically ambitious used car salesman depicted by William H. Macy, begins to have second thoughts regarding his ill-formed kidnapping plot, he goes to visit Shep Proudfoot, his underworld connection. When he asks how he can get in touch with Showalter and Grimsrud, the kidnappers he hired to abduct his wife, Shep points out that he only made the connection with one: "Put you in touch with Grimsrud." "Well, yah," Jerry replies, "but he had a buddy there." "Well, I don't vouch for him," Shep says. "Never heard of him. Don't vouch for him."

AN INVENTION WITHOUT A FUTURE

Even the worst movie has much of the authority of the actual, and quite without knowing it one comes out of the theater brainwashed into scanning the world through the norms of the camera [...] the moviegoer walks about taking shots and sequences unaware.
—Richard Wilbur[2]

A genre is a vision of the world. It tells us what kinds of people the world is populated by, what motivates them, how they typically interact,

---

2   Richard Wilbur, "Movies and Dreams," in *The Catbird's Song: Prose Pieces 1963–1995*, (Harcourt, Brace, 1997), p. 153.

which ones ought to be running the show and which ones need to be kept in line. It tells us what counts as a meaningful resolution, what counts as an appropriate ending to a story. The hero prevails. The dual protagonists get married. The mystery is solved. The estranged relatives overcome their misunderstandings and achieve a reconciliation. The wrongdoers are brought to justice. The journeyer returns home, wiser than before. Order is restored to the cosmos.

Fargo is somewhat less overt than many Coen films in its deployment of genre mechanisms, its directors retreating mostly into the blizzard-blanked background, presenting a naturistically told tale, allegedly based on real events, about a crime gone wrong and the dogged investigator who cracks the case. But terms like *naturalism* and *realism* are themselves indications of style and, depending on the context, of genre. Roland Barthes wrote of being afflicted with "a feeling of impatience at the sight of the 'naturalness' with which newspapers, art, and common sense constantly dress up a reality which, even though it is the one we live in, is undoubtedly determined by history." The result of this affliction was that Barthes "wanted to track down, in the decorative display of *what-goes-without-saying*, the ideological abuse which, in my view, is hidden there."[3] It is impossible to view a film properly—that is, intelligently, wakefully, with awareness—without keeping in mind the fact that the "decorative display" of a film does not only reveal but also conceals, and that part of what is concealed is always ideological in nature.

True story. True crime film. Based on real events. One of the things *Fargo* accomplishes—not so much within its frame as in its troublesome and troubling dealings with external reality—is to remind us that, like the claim that a film is "naturalistic" or "realistic," phrases like these

---

3   Roland Barthes, *Mythologies* (trans. Annette Lavers, Hill & Wang, 1972), pp. 10–11.

are no guarantee that a sequence of events is in fact being depicted "exactly as it occurred." To make us wonder, indeed, what this would *be*, what it would look like, what it could possibly *mean* to present, in two hours or less, on a two-dimensional screen, a real-world sequence of events "exactly as it occurred."

The Lumière brothers, those pioneers of early cinema technology, regarded film as a novelty, "an invention without any future." All that film did, they reasoned, was to show people things they could see for themselves anyway: people walking, eating, performing the actions of ordinary life. The many reasons why people might turn out to have an inexhaustible hunger for such images did not, it seems, occur to them. That the very act of putting something on a screen might make it fascinating in a way that ordinary events taking place before our eyes might not be. That there was a kind of gratification in the one-way transactions of film viewership, of seeing images of people who could not look back at you. Perhaps they also forgot that the camera could be pointed at exotic and unusual things, things we would not otherwise be able to see. And that unusual and exotic things, things that had no existence outside of the realm of cinema, could be *created* for the camera, as Georges Méliès and others would soon do. That things that existed outside of the realm of cinema could be presented, on screen, as if they were as real as people talking, eating, and performing the everyday actions of ordinary human life.

Filmed images can reveal truth, by showing that something happened. They can serve as evidence. Yet we are all by now used to filmed images that do no such thing. Georges Méliès' *A Trip to the Moon* (1902) did not prove that there were people who had actually taken a trip to the moon. And despite the opening admonition that they tell a true story, the images that compose *Fargo* do not establish that events of the sort depicted took place in Minnesota in 1987, or at any time. A posed picture, a recording of a staged episode, proves no more than does a painting; **39** it is a record of something that is itself concocted, designed to suggest an event that likely never took place. But the human brain is wired to believe what it sees, even if, intellectually, we know that the image we are seeing is the recording of something staged, or a special effect. Being seen gives a thing a pretense of reality, what Richard Wilbur calls "the authority of the actual." We believe what we see, and we neglect, or forget, whatever is covered over and concealed by the seen thing. Even if the seen thing is a mere fiction, while what is concealed, what we are prevented from seeing, is reality.

OUT OF RESPECT FOR THE DEAD

> *People can't get enough of them, the familiar stories, like little children. Because they connect the stories to themselves, I suppose. And we all love hearing about ourselves, over and over. So long as the people in the story are—us but not us.*
>
> —Thigpen, *The Ballad of Buster Scruggs*

What we are largely prevented from seeing, in *Fargo*, is a human being who stands somewhere near the center of things: Jean Lundegaard. Jerry's wife, the kidnapping victim. Who talks about her afterward, who remembers her? She is rarely onscreen. When she is, her face is frequently covered. She gets just a few lines of innocuous dialogue. In a film whose primary themes include visibility and concealment, the invisibility of Jean Lundegaard demands a level of attention it is highly unlikely to receive.

The glimpses we are granted of Jean's ordinary life are tragically brief. The last of those glimpses finds her seated comfortably at home, watching television, happily absorbing one of those dumb artificial morning news and chat programs. The program is inane, and she seems

40 to be enjoying it precisely as she is intended to, taking it at face value, charmed and reassured by the empty patter of the onscreen hosts. We might well be tempted to read a great deal into this, to form judgments of her character, her entire personality, on the basis of these few seconds. As a result of this, combined with the silence and invisibility soon to be imposed on her by her kidnappers, we may well relegate her to the category of "unworthy victim"—to borrow a term from Edward Herman and Noam Chomsky's *Manufacturing Consent* (1988). This will limit the sympathy we feel for her, and the degree to which we can engage with her. We will be, as we frequently are when watching crime dramas, not to mention the news, more caught up in the details of the crime itself, the behavior of the perpetrators, and the facts about how they are ultimately brought to justice, than with the suffering of the victims of crimes. The fact that bringing the kidnappers to justice does nothing to restore Jean to life, and hence cannot in any way restore a prior order or return the universe to a kind of cosmic balance, is likely to go unmentioned, one of the sad facts of human existence that rarely makes it to the screen.

Did Jerry understand, when he hired these two brutal thugs, that the result was that something would actually happen? That events would transpire, that people would be hurt? That his *wife* would almost certainly be grievously harmed? (But if Jean is invisible to all of us, she is especially so to her husband.) One senses that when Jerry imagined how things would play out, he did so in terms and images that he picked up from the movies. Jerry, after all, seems to live his life as if it were a movie. Do we ever see him not acting? Perhaps his only authentic act or utterance is the scream he emits at the end when he is finally apprehended. Until then we know him only through the roles he plays, relative to whoever might be in the room with him. Talking with Showalter and Grimsrud, he tries to portray himself as a criminal mastermind,

a man who is in control and who has thought things through. Soon **41**
after we find him putting on a little pageant for two customers who
have made the mistake of buying a car from him, pretending to consult
the manager about an expensive, unwanted, valueless application of
"TruCoat" sealant, while doing no such thing. (Given the film's concern
with truth and concealment, the name of the "TruCoat" surely can't
help but strike us as metaphorically resonant.)

Later we find Jerry preparing to phone Jean's father, Wade Gustafson,
to deliver the news of Jean's abduction. Like any good actor, he is
preparing for his big scene, rehearsing his lines, making sure his delivery
will be smooth and his tone will be just right. That scene turns out to
be a precursor for a later one involving Wade himself. Having rejected
Jerry's firm insistence that he go alone to deliver the ransom—"They
were real clear about that," Jerry says of the kidnappers—Wade decides
that he will take them the money himself. It is, after all, his money.
Wade, it appears, has also seen a lot of movies: John Wayne Westerns,
Clint Eastwood's *Dirty Harry* movies, that sort of thing. In his mind,
all it takes is a firm, authoritative figure with a gun to bring vigilante
justice to the lawbreakers. In his car, on his way to meet Carl Showalter,
steering with one hand while practicing with his pistol—he wants the
delivery of his bullet, should he be required to shoot, to be as smooth
as the delivery of his dialogue—Wade does what Jerry did before him:
he rehearses his lines. "Okay, here's your money—now where's my
damn daughter? Goddamn punk—where my damn daughter? You little
punk." (As Richard Wilbur writes, "The mannerisms of movie stars,
unconsciously borrowed and recognized without specific reminiscence,
have for us something of the universality of the Italian vocabulary of
gestures, though of course they are more transitory."[4])

---

4   Wilbur, "Movies and Dreams," p. 153.

42 The Coens' films are often characterized as "self-conscious" and "ironic." While this is frequently true of the films, we should be clear that it is *not* true of most of the Coens' characters. If they behave as if they were characters in a movie, it is because they inhabit a society in which the pervasiveness of media, and in particular of cinematic narratives, has so penetrated people's experience that most people think of themselves, and of life, in the terms set by those media and narratives. And because Coen plots tend to obey not the narrative logic of commercial film, but something closer to the causal logic of actual life, these characters nearly inevitably end up surprised and disappointed. Almost tragically so. Like Jerry, surveying the wreckage of his plans, screaming in outrage and incomprehension as he is apprehended, believing with all his heart that this wasn't the way it was supposed to end. Or Wade Gustafson, shot through his very puffy, very cozy-looking parka, falling to his knees before his executioner, Carl Showalter, and—having been at long last brought face to face with irrefutable reality—uttering his final words, the same words Jerry Lundegaard will utter a few minutes later when he finds his father-in-law's still-warm corpse in the snow:

"Oh, geez."

Oh, geez. The final words of a man who has at last been forced to confront a reality that had been previously screened off from him by his money, his power, his entertainments and comforts. Who has, in a sense, gotten what he wanted. He didn't want to send Jerry as his emissary. He wanted to handle things himself. He wanted to see the men who had kidnapped his daughter, and were trying to take his money, with his own eyes.

TECHNOLOGY DROVE THE MESSAGE

People don't want the facts! They want to believe!
—Eddie Mannix, *Hail, Caesar!*

THE FIXERS

I don't care it's true, it's not true; it stinks!
—Freddy Riedenschneider, *The Man Who Wasn't There*

43

In his book *Excellent Sheep: The Miseducation of the American Elite,* William Deresiewicz tells the story of a young woman who, having left college after a single semester, dismissed the value of education by saying that in the real world, "No one cares how well you can talk about Hume or Kant." Deresiewicz's response—that people in the real world *do* care about how well you can talk and think, which are the primary skills honed by liberal education—is true enough, but it concedes a bit too much. I wish he had said that the "no one" is a serious overstatement: that in fact, there are quite a few people in the world—and not only in universities—who *do* care how well you can talk about Hume and Kant. You can, of course, choose to construct a life in which there is no one, least of all yourself, who cares about Hume or Kant, or history, or science, or any other element of intellect or culture. People do choose to live such lives. But even more people, I suspect, end up in such lives by default, not because they have chosen them but because they got the message from every quarter that that sort of life—the sort of life where there is nothing serious to think about, where we need not use our brains for anything other than figuring out what to have for dinner tonight and what to watch on whatever streaming service happens to be available to us—is the norm, the default. It's how *everybody* lives.

Claims about what "no one" cares about, or what "everybody" knows or thinks, or how "everyone" lives, are curiously common, given that pretty much every one of them is false. Human experiences, beliefs, and ways of living are extraordinarily diverse. Once, after discussing a case of a young woman who became pregnant because she had never been taught that sex leads to pregnancy, a student in my ethics class insisted to me that the story could not possibly be true, because "there isn't anybody who doesn't know that." Like all of us, this student was saddled with an imperfect piece of thinking equipment, a human brain. And the human brain is a remarkably effective—indeed, *excessively* effective—generalization machine. Given a story about one person it will leap to the conclusion that that's how things are for everyone. And because it's the most effective way of reaching the largest possible audience, this generalization mechanism is indulged and encouraged by the majority of television and internet content, which endorses and replicates the notion that there are things that *everyone* is interested in and other things that no one on the planet cares about. It is a basic advertising strategy, after all, to convince you that everyone has, or wants, the latest product; from which it is supposed to follow that you, too, need it, and need it very badly.

On the other hand, because most people *don't* care whether you can talk about Hume or Kant, or Locke or Rousseau, you won't, for the most part, hear references to those philosophers, or any other recondite subject matter, on the evening news, or on most entertainment programs. ("The Good Place" being, of course, the exception that proves the rule.) Never mind that their thinking has shaped the culture we live in, to the extent where genuine self-knowledge—a full understanding of why you think and feel and see things the way you do—is impossible to those who are entirely unfamiliar with their writings. The references you encounter on television, or on any medium that aims itself at the masses, will be to things the producers believe everyone is familiar with, things that won't alienate anybody or make anyone uncomfortable by suggesting there might be things that we *don't* know yet, which are nonetheless important to know. Which further encourages the perception that everyone thinks, knows, believes, and is interested in the same things. And that most of those things are in fact quite shallow, apparent, and easy to understand, and have to do, either directly or indirectly, either with consumer goods or celebrity culture.

That generalizing machine that is your brain is always hard at work. People think everyone—or everyone *normal,* anyway—speaks the language they speak, eats the foods they eat. People who watch a lot of TV think everyone watches a lot of TV. People who don't know anyone who voted for Joe Biden will think, there's no way that election was fair. *No one* voted for Biden. Not a single person in my Facebook feed. And if everyone we see thinks it's supremely important to buy a new car every two years or so, we might think that everyone thinks that. Even if a lot of those people we see, who have that attitude, are on TV. Characters in car commercials, perhaps. Or characters in the TV programs that are paid for by car commercials.

Suppose you don't live in a city, but that whenever you see the people who inhabit cities, everyone you see there is either a drug user, or a drug dealer, or someone who lives in fear of the drug users and drug dealers. Maybe these people we're talking about, the people you are generalizing from, aren't actual residents of cities at all—maybe you never go to cities, largely because you're frightened of the drugs and the violent crime—but they're people on TV. And maybe those poor people living in fear remind you of yourself, whereas the drug users and drug dealers don't. They talk different. They dress different. We won't mention the color of their skin. During the past few decades the American public has experienced wave after wave of media-fed fear: fear of drugs and drug users, fear of child abusers, fear of random carjackings, muggings, and kidnappings, fear of the monstrous violent offenders John DiIulio, Frederic Fox Leadership Professor of Politics, Religion, and Civil Society at the University of Pennsylvania, termed "superpredators" in the '90s. Millions of Americans became convinced, and continue to believe, that the country was under siege by a horde of terrifying, unpredictably violent thugs. People from elsewhere, people who didn't share our American values, and who posed a threat to us.

46 It's a myth—unsupported by actual statistics—that Donald Trump appealed to, to great effect, in his 2016 presidential campaign, and has continued to promote ever since.

The image of an assailing horde of dangerous, hyper-violent criminals got into people's heads, into people's dreams. We see this, in television news reporting and other news media, again and again. If a certain sort of story gets consistently reported, viewers believe this happens all the time; that it is the norm, it is what happens, it is what is happening to people like them. Seeing is believing. You see a crackhead on the screen, or a victim of a mugging, and you immediately jump to the belief that much of the country's population consists of criminals and victims. Unsurprisingly, perhaps, studies tell us that a person's beliefs regarding the extent and likelihood of crime are correlated with the amount of local TV news they watch. The more televised news they consume, the more violent they believe the world to be.

In his book *The Age of the Image,* Stephen Apkon writes, with reference to the 1991 police beating of Rodney King:

"To be 'real' enough to be taken seriously, the event had to be *seen.* We had to *see* Officer Powell's baton striking the hapless King, to *see* those vicious baton blows being administered to a fallen man [...] Those who were paying attention knew all about the abuses of the LAPD in the African American community [...] But it took a video to galvanize the public at large, bringing a visceral emotional capstone to a mountain of written material. The video made it all 'real.' [...] The ideology did not drive the message. *Technology* drove the message."[5]

In the eight years since Apkon wrote this, the reaction by millions of right-leaning Americans to the Black Lives Matter protests has

---

5   Stephen Apkon, *The Age of the Image: Redefining Literacy in a World of Screens* (Farrar, Straus, Giroux, 2013), pp. 107-8.

demonstrated that a lot of people have been receiving a rather different technology-driven message. In some respects what has happened is a replay of events that took place in the '60s, when Republican politicians and the media aligned with them managed to portray racial justice protests as uncontrolled, violent riots that threatened to engulf the entire country. Similarly, Republican TV and internet ads during the 2020 election showed images of towns, neighborhoods, and flags on fire, and portrayed Democrats as inviting and supporting chaos and violent mob rule. That many of these advertisements used irrelevant or decontextualized footage to encourage a highly misleading perception of what was actually taking place didn't stop these images from galvanizing a large portion of the viewing (and voting) public. But this time around, of course, the effect was dramatically exacerbated by the internet, and in particular by the epistemic bubbles and echo chambers of social media. The tendency of social media algorithms to provide users with stories and experiences that reflect and reinforce the beliefs and values they already hold—encouraging the perception that everybody thinks what you think and knows what you know, or, if there are any who disagree, that they must be uninformed, perverse, and likely a threat—would have been dangerous even if no one had thought to deliberately exploit it for political purposes. In the hands of skillful media manipulators it has become downright toxic—a toxicity we are still trying to figure out how to expel from our system.

"To be 'real' enough to be taken seriously, the event had to be seen." Indeed. But just what is it that is seen, when technology duplicates and distributes an image? What the viewer thinks they are seeing is itself often determined by ideology. Maybe technology is driving the message. But if the content of the message is ideologically determined, that fact is hardly reassuring.

OH, GEEZ

Hell, I could tell you some stories—
—Charlie Meadows, *Barton Fink*

It had been five or six years since I had last watched *Fargo*, and I was struck on this latest viewing by just how much Wade Gustafson resembled Donald Trump. It was mid-November, a little more than a week since Joe Biden had been declared the election's winner, and we were all, perhaps, just beginning to wonder exactly how long Trump would go on spinning stories about victory and fraud, stories that bore no relation to reality but which were eagerly accepted as reality by tens of millions of Americans. And there, on my screen in the midst of all this, was Wade, a blunt, cartoonish figure, all bluster, swagger, and empty self-assurance, whose conceit and combative disparagement of those around him seems intended to conceal how little lies underneath. As a man whose vision of the world seems derived from Hollywood movies, he has, unsurprisingly, cast himself in the role of action hero or sheriff. When Jerry insists that they obey the kidnappers' instructions that he himself deliver the money, and that he do so alone, Wade will hear nothing of it. In his mind he must be the one to make the delivery. It is, after all, his damn daughter. And more importantly, it's his damn money.

Casting yourself in the role of the cowboy, the Western hero, is a longstanding American tradition. It's a move that makes sense in American politics, given how strongly our view of the world tends to be shaped by the values and presuppositions of those films. In a 1972 interview, Henry Kissinger offered Oriana Fallaci the following explanation of his popularity:

"The main point … in the mechanics of my success comes from the fact that I have acted alone. The Americans love this immensely. The Americans love the cowboy, who leads the convoy, alone on his horse, the cowboy who comes into town all alone on his horse, and nothing else…. He acts, and that is enough, being in the right place at the right time. In sum, a Western. This romantic and surprising character suits me because being alone has always been part of my style, or, if you wish, of my technique."

The cowboy, like the revolutionary, works outside the system. For Americans, doing things yourself is how you know things are done right. When there's no one around you can trust, you can still always trust yourself. Self-doubt, self-criticism, self-examination: these are not touted as American virtues. The standard set of American virtues include self-reliance, self-confidence, self-assurance, and self-promotion. Moreover, in a highly mediated world, the idea of bypassing the media, looking *around* the screen, in order to check reality itself, has an undeniable appeal. How would Wade ever know what had really gone down on the rooftop of that parking garage if he had to take Jerry's word for it? He wanted to see things with his own eyes.

Checking it out in person, running the experiment for yourself: this idea is at the heart of Enlightenment science, and of the American inheritance from the Enlightenment. But when combined with other elements of the American mindset—in particular, our distrust of authority, which more and more has combined with anti-intellectualism, hostility toward expertise, political paranoia, and a bizarre gullibility directed toward the outlandish claims of those who, in rejecting the pronouncements of traditional authorities, set themselves up as the "real" authorities—the results can be toxic.

Thus, in 2016, when rumors were spreading across the more credulous segments of the internet that Hillary Clinton and other high-level Democrats were running a child slavery ring out of a pizzeria in Washington, D.C. (it was alleged that children were being held in the tunnels beneath the pizzeria), Edgar Welch, of Salisbury, North

 Carolina, did what, under other circumstances, Wade Gustafson might have done: he got his gun, got into his car, and drove to the scene of the (purported) crime, to see the truth with his own eyes. The truth, of course, was that nothing was going on, but it wasn't until after he had fired his assault rifle inside the pizzeria, in order to open a locked door that impeded his investigation, that that truth began, in a somewhat minimal way, to dawn on him.

Welch had recently had internet installed at his house, which had allowed him, as he told reporters in an interview published three days after his arrest, to "really look into it"—"it" being the allegations regarding Clinton and the pizzeria. He wanted to "take a closer look" and "shine some light on it." After all, somebody said there were captive kids in that pizzeria, and whoever it was, it was someone on the internet, not part of the untrustworthy media elite. According to the *Washington Post*, as he drove he "texted his girlfriend a Bible verse about being anointed by God." He stated in the same interview that during the drive to D.C. his heart was "breaking over the thought of innocent people suffering."[6]

As far as the allegations themselves, his failure to find any evidence at the site convinced him only that there were no children being held at that time at that particular location. (There are, after all, a lot of other pizzerias in D.C.) "The intel on this," as he rather mildly put it to the reporters, "wasn't 100 percent correct." Neither this admission, nor the thorough debunking of the conspiracy theory that followed, prevented the pizzeria's owners from receiving multiple death threats from others who also believed the internet rumors. Nor did it prevent

---

6   Spencer Hsu, "'Pizzagate' Gunman Says He Was Foolish, Reckless, Mistaken—and Sorry." *Washington Post*, June 14 , 2017. https://www.washingtonpost.com/local/public-safety/pizzagate-shooter-apologizes-in-handwritten-letter-for-his-mistakes-ahead-of-sentencing/2017/06/13/f35126b6-5086-11e7-be25-3a519335381c_story.html Accessed December 13, 2020.

Michael Flynn's son—who, like his father, was at the time a member of Donald Trump's transition team—from tweeting, "Until #Pizzagate proven to be false, it'll remain a story."

Hillary Clinton abuses kids in the basement of a D.C. pizzeria: true story? Well, I can't vouch for it. But it sure does make a good story.

Let's face it: we Americans love our stories. The story of a lone protagonist getting his gun and getting in his car—or, in the more romantic old days, getting on his horse—and heading out to find the truth and set things right, guided only by his individual conscience and with no help from the established authorities, remains a favorite.

It's because of our foundational attachment to such stories that the automobile constitutes such a paradigmatically *American* piece of technology. Its main innovation is not its speed, but its isolation, the fact that it lets us carry with us our own little environment, our own little world. A world in which I control the temperature—keeping me toasty warm even while blizzards rage outside—and can tune into the talk radio station that reflects my own values and beliefs. Like all our favorite technologies—cell phones, AirPods, social media platforms, handguns—the automobile allows me to construct a private world according to my private desires and values, and to express and, when push comes to shove, enforce those values with ruthless efficiency.

Perhaps there is part of us that should sympathize with Wade Gustafson in his confusion and lack of self-awareness, a man who, in heading to his doom, is only doing what his culture has trained him from the beginning to do. Perhaps we would, if we thought he was more concerned about the fate of his daughter than the fate of his money.

Poor Wade. So puffed up and hollow that when he is shot he doesn't even bleed blood. Only feathers.

  THE INTEL ON THIS WASN'T 100 PERCENT CORRECT

What happens when everybody owns a television set?
—Cuddahy, *Hail, Caesar!*

We ain't one-at-a-timin' here! We mass communicatin'!
—Pappy O'Daniel, *O Brother, Where Art Thou?*

Who vouches for the stories told on TV news programs, the stories we read online? On TV, the presence of a person, a newscaster, with a recognizable face, might make us feel, indeed is intended to make us feel, that here is someone to be trusted. Someone we know, someone who would never mislead us. And behind this friendly face, what? How many boardrooms, how many producers, scriptwriters, advertisers, decision-makers? And behind the blog, or the voice in the YouTube video, intoning dire interpretations over almost random images, who? A real person? A single person? A group of people? How large? Headquartered where? With what agenda? Are we reassured, or all the more suspicious, if it is a single person, a lone voice, as opposed to a group?

It might have been hoped—it *was* hoped, by some, for a while—that the communal and democratic nature of the internet, the fact that it now takes so little to start a blog, to post a comment, to upload a video, would somehow bring about a better, more inclusive, more informative public discourse. Isn't the very accessibility of such resources the antidote to the sorts of censorship and screening inherent in television, or the movies, or print publishing, where a significant financial investment is necessary in order to participate? Wouldn't the internet constitute a free marketplace of ideas, in which the intellectual cream would rise to the top, as John Stuart Mill predicted? But what floated to the top, mostly, was skewed political material, unreadable clickbait, and cat videos. The expanding grip of conspiracy theories like Pizzagate and

QAnon ought, by now, to have extirpated any lingering hope that the online world would provide a new and clearer portal to the truth.

It's hard to say exactly why the internet seems so much *more* amenable to the rapid promulgation of conspiracy theories and related lies, rumors, and outright malarkey than the media that had preceded it. Unless, of course, one takes a despairing view and holds that it is precisely *because* it is more democratic, precisely *because* the bars to access are so low. The gates are open to anyone with an agenda, including those whose only agenda is to fuck with you by making you believe something that isn't true, or doubt something that is. Not to mention the self-appointed experts on politics or, well, anything at all, who in earlier times would have been laughed out of the room had they tried to publish their fantasies or broadcast them on TV. As a result, it is natural for the paranoid-but-credulous to see the internet as open to all, as democratic in a positive sense, as providing truths heretofore suppressed with a place to go.

Never mind that there are just as many videos and websites out there claiming, and proclaiming, the opposite of whatever truth the internet has just revealed to you. Americans have always believed—it's part of the intellectual inheritance from Protestantism that has shaped American ways of thinking about belief and truth—that in their heart of hearts they can discern the truth, they can *feel* it. And sometimes, of course, it works. A video of police brutality can go viral in hours, sometimes minutes, and provoke public outrage. But a QAnon video, or a misleading political ad, can go viral just as quickly, and have just as persuasive an effect on the brains that have been primed to believe it. Especially if in some deep way it taps in to the subconscious myths we as a people have absorbed: myths about our exceptionalism and innocence, our being besieged on all sides (including from within) by impure invaders, about our only hope lying in virtuous action exercised

54 by lone individuals acting for the most part outside the purview of official institutions and recognized authorities. The kinds of myths, that is, that animate the Western genre.

Wade Gustafson is surely delusional in casting himself as a heroic sheriff figure; but there is no denying that *Fargo* is largely structured like a Western. Two strangers ride into town, kill a bunch of innocent folks, nab a hostage, and head out for the hills, leaving it to a heroic lawman—well, lawwoman, in this case—to hunt them down, at significant risk to herself, and bring them to justice. Much of the action, and many of the killings, take place away from town, out in the open, small human bodies committing acts of violence under yawning, indifferent skies. All in all, it was only natural that Wade Gustafson would cast himself as a Western hero, a righteous vigilante out to bring evildoers to justice.

As American film genres, the Western and the *film noir* are central. The former purports to tell the story of how an untamed land was settled, the latter revels in the seedy corruption and moral sickness that sprouted afterward in the settled places. These are, of course, films made by and for the descendants of Europeans; you aren't going to get a true account, from most Westerns, of the treatment of those who already inhabited this continent at the hands of white folks; and the very idea that North America was not settled until it was tamed by Europeans is a wildly slanted history, more myth than fact. As a genre, the Western always evokes the unavoidable question of what is being concealed—of which stories are not being told, which are being buried under the stories that are, beneath the visible images projected on the screen.

In a Western, if you are a just man, and you hear of an injustice, you get your gun, and you get on your horse, and you ride out to see where the trouble is. To see what's what with your own eyes, and find out if your intel was a hundred percent accurate. And then you act, to rescue the endangered innocent, to right what's wrong. In *Fargo*, Marge

Gunderson does this, as does Sheriff Ed Tom in *No Country for Old Men*; and, in her way, Mattie Ross in *True Grit*. Though Ed Tom, for his part, is getting tired of this, he almost can't get himself up on the old horse anymore. He feels in his bones that the world has changed, though likely it's never been the way the stories told him it ought to be. Whatever myths they might have been premised on, the classic American Westerns told a story of righteousness triumphant; they may have indulged in grave distortions in their relations with reality, but within their own self-contained cosmos the good guys behaved well and won out, in the end, over the bad. There is a part of Sheriff Ed Tom that believes those stories. But *No Country for Old Men*, like *Fargo*, does not inhabit that universe. Like the world itself, though, it is populated in large part by people who believe that they do.

IT'S TRUE THAT IT'S A STORY

> *The math tells how it really works. That's the real thing. The stories I give you in class are just illustrative; they're like, fables, say, to help give you a picture. An imperfect model. I mean, even I don't understand the dead cat.*
>
> —Larry Gopnik, *A Serious Man*

That dead cat, of course, belonged—inasmuch as a fictional feline can belong to anyone— to Erwin Schrödinger, part of the famous thought experiment he offered Albert Einstein to explain his discomfort with the Copenhagen interpretation of quantum physics. In an earlier Coen film, *The Man Who Wasn't There*, the lawyer Freddy Riedenschneider appeals to quantum physics—specifically, Heisenberg's Uncertainty Principle—to create the reasonable doubt that gets his clients exonerated. As Riedenschneider sees matters, if the physicists are right then everything that happens in this world is a matter of reasonable doubt,

56 and no one can be convicted or held responsible for anything. (For his part, Larry Gopnik, who teaches physics at a community college, resists this conclusion, acknowledging that "the Uncertainty Principle ... proves we can't ever really know what's going on," but adding, "But even though you can't figure anything out, you'll still be responsible for it on the midterm.")

Uncertainty is a constant presence and theme in Coen films. The Uncertainty Principle and Schrödinger's Cat are both alluded to in *Inside Llewyn Davis* (2013), a film about split histories and alternative possibilities. In the fifth segment of *The Ballad of Buster Scruggs* (2018), Billy Knapp voices one of the film's key lines to the mildly mousy yet desirable Alice Longabaugh: "Uncertainty—that is appropriate for the matters of this world." A little more than a decade earlier Sheriff Ed Tom, in *No Country for Old Men*, had said to Carla Jean Moss, "Even in the contest between man and steer, the issue is not certain." His line was the culmination of a story about a man they both knew, Charlie Walser. But would Charlie Walser have vouched for it? The real punch line to the story comes later in the film, when Carla Jean challenges Ed Tom, asking him if the story was in fact true. "True story?" says Ed Tom, who barely even remembers telling it. "Well, I couldn't swear to every detail. But it's certainly true that it's a story."

Which returns us to *Fargo's* themes of visibility and concealment. Think of Jerry at the beginning of the film, squinting through his snow-stricken windshield. Later, when he tries to scrape the ice off that frozen windshield, he flies into a frustrated rage. Things will never be clear for Jerry, and on some level he knows it. Think of Grimsrud, peering through the glass into Jean Lundegaard's living room, into the sort of house, and life, he cannot imagine inhabiting. Speaking of rage, think of Carl Showalter, pounding on his TV set, trying to clear it of the snow that prevents him from seeing anything in the only world—the tiny, contained, artificial world of television—he and Grimsrud can understand or feel anything for. Later, out in the snow—the other kind of snow—having buried the suitcase full of money, Showalter realizes that he will not be able to find it again, that the blankness of the blizzard and the enormity of the landscape will rob him of the prize he has bought with so much blood. To prevent this, to try to win a victory over the void, he performs a laughably futile gesture, planting a blood-red windshield scraper in the snow to mark where the treasure has been buried. As if that tiny mark lost in a blank white field could render things visible, as it if could resolve the inevitable uncertainty of where the money had been hidden.

I had a fortune and I lost it in the snow. Now there's a story that we can believe. It won't matter, in the end; Showalter will never get the chance to return and try to locate the money. He himself will be reduced to a red mark in the snow, when his partner murders him in a dispute over the car, the tan Ciera they got from Jerry Lundegaard. Having cheated Grimsrud out of the majority of the ransom money, you would think he could let him have the car, that he could let it go. But his self-righteous fury renders him incapable of letting anything go. Grimsrud dispatches Showalter with an axe, then begins to feed his body through the woodchipper out back. As if gripped with the desire to erase history, to cover, to conceal. To make the world blank. Just what Showalter, in his way, was trying to prevent.

The great advantage of a blank world, of course, is that we can write on it whatever story we want. Like Jerry Lundegaard, spinning his endless lies, his cycle of tales in which he plays the role of the thing he is furthest from being in actual life: a decent, honest, and capable human being. Those sprawling blank fields of Minnesotan snow—they remind us (we can't keep from making the association) of a movie screen, the blank void onto which our stories are projected. The blankness into

58 which our cameras are pointed. "We tell ourselves stories in order to live," Joan Didion famously wrote in *The White Album*, which could have been an alternate title for *Fargo*.[7] But we might also say: we tell ourselves stories in order to keep other stories from being told.

Late in *No Country for Old Men*, Llewellyn Moss finds himself in a telephone conversation with Anton Chigurh, the unstoppable, remorseless killer who more or less represents Death Himself. "I've decided to make you a special project of mine," he tells Chigurh. "You ain't going to have to look for me at all." Llewellyn, too, seems to have slipped into the delusion that he is the hero of some action film, and that all the action around him is tending toward a final, climactic showdown. (His otherwise sensible wife seems to share some of that delusion, rendering her unable to properly heed Sheriff Ed Tom's warnings. Told that Llewellyn is in trouble with some killers who won't quit, she replies, "He won't neither. He never has. He can take all comers.")

Many viewers let themselves slip into that same delusion, which is why so many people felt disappointed, and in some cases betrayed, when the plot went in a very different direction, ending with a thoughtful soliloquy by Sheriff Ed Tom, who slumps at his table and describes his dreams from the night before. As for Moss, not only does he fail to defeat Chigurh, and not only does he fail to survive; he never even finds Chigurh, and the dramatic confrontation between the two of them never takes place. When he dies an inglorious death *offscreen*, it finally dawns on the viewer that he was never the center of the film. Rather, the film has no center. In that way, it resembles the world.

"We look for the sermon in the suicide," Didion writes, "for the social or moral lesson in the murder of five. We interpret what we see, select the most workable of the multiple choices. We live entirely,

---

7   Joan Didion, *The White Album*, p. 11.

especially if we are writers, by the imposition of a narrative line upon disparate images, by the 'ideas' with which we have learned to freeze the shifting phantasmagoria which is our actual experience."[8] Like Larry Gopnik in the Coens' *A Serious Man* (2009), we insist on believing that every story, even a story as overtly nonsensical as the story of "the goy's teeth," must be trying to tell us something. Hopefully something reassuring. Like Llewellyn Moss, each of us places ourselves in the central, heroic role of the narrative we take to constitute the universe. Watching *Fargo*, we identify with Marge Gunderson, not pausing to ask whether we might find a truer reflection in the hapless Jerry, or the uncontrolled and raging Carl Showalter. Indeed, the truth is that many of us might most resemble one of the bit players: Marge's goofy police partner; her husband, who hopes his bird paintings will end up on a stamp; the barely acknowledged, barely visible Jean Lundegaard.

It's foolish to think that your life is a film, or enough like a film that certain things are assured of working out, that certain securities are guaranteed, that certain good intentions will necessarily bear fruit. That you, or certain parts of you, or of your life, are immune to the workings of fate and chance, because the Great Screenwriter in the Sky will write the plot so that you come out alright in the end. It's foolish to believe, like Chad Feldheimer and Linda Litzke in *Burn After Reading* (2008), that if you have seen a few crime and caper films you know enough about how the world works to successfully blackmail a CIA agent. It's foolish to think, like Mattie Ross in *True Grit* (2010), that the righteousness of your cause will guarantee that you'll prevail in the struggle against experienced killers. Mattie is yet another Wade figure, with her horse and her gun, in love with a myth of justice she has concocted out of hearsay and Bible stories, riding off on a quest to

59

---

8   Joan Didion, *The White Album*, p. 11.

 confront the evildoers and continue the taming of the West. What is most foolish about Mattie, of course, is her insistence that she herself be the agent who brings Tom Chaney to justice. It isn't enough for her that he be tried and convicted; he has to be convicted of the crime that matters to her, the murder of her father. Just putting him in prison—or even executing him—is not, for her, enough. For all her precocious intelligence and maturity, Mattie still holds a view of justice in which it is always possible to restore the world to a perfectly balanced and just state, as long as the proper acts, most of which involve the punishment of those who perpetrate injustice, are performed. But then, there are a lot of adults who buy that sort of story, too. They believe it, probably, because they've watched too much television, or seen too many movies. Or maybe, like Mattie Ross, they've read too many Bible stories.

THE DECORATIVE DISPLAY OF WHAT GOES WITHOUT SAYING

The more you look, the less you really know. It's a fact, a true fact.
In a way, it's the only fact there is.
—Freddy Riedenschneider, *The Man Who Wasn't There*

Do you see me?
—Anton Chigurh, *No Country for Old Men*

There isn't always a lesson. The imposed narrative line nearly always falsifies. But the line between the view that the truth is complex, and the view that there just isn't any truth beyond what people are willing to accept and enforce, seems harder and harder for people to grasp. The latter view constitutes a radical skepticism that leads straight to the conclusion that anything goes, that whatever story is loudest, or most entertaining, or has the most money behind it, will win the right to be referred to as "the truth." This is the view promoted by the title character of *The Big Lebowski. Not* the Dude, though people sometimes make that mistake; I mean the *other* Jeffrey Lebowski, the one with the opulent house and the big swimming pool. The Dude is no skeptic; when he says, "Well, that's just, like, your opinion, man," his point is that some expressions of belief are *only* that, opinion. The facts don't back them up. Whereas, when the "big" Lebowski says to the Dude, "You have your story, I have mine," he is expressing the cynical view that it doesn't *matter* whether the facts back your story up. What's more important is that the cops back you up, or that the lawyers do, or Newsmax, or whatever internet commentator has the attention of this week's credulous mob. The truth is that whoever has the money on their side more or less gets to say what the truth is.

Some characters in Coen films strive to make the truth visible. Think of the detective characters: Marge in *Fargo*, the Dude in *Lebowski*, Sheriff Ed Tom in *No Country*, and the various other investigators, private eyes, and journalists who pop up here and there in their *oeuvre*. Others strive to make themselves visible, or maintain the visibility they have achieved: creative artists like the titular characters of *Barton Fink* and *Inside Llewyn Davis*, and the various actors in *Hail, Caesar!* Some, like Jean Lundegaard, have invisibility violently imposed upon them. Those who desire invisibility are frequently criminals: murderers, blackmailers, kidnappers, gangsters, along with assorted adulterers, spies, and behind-the-scenes manipulators and businessmen. And some characters strive for visibility and invisibility in the same moment. Llewyn Davis struggles to be seen by audiences and promoters while hiding the fact that he is sleeping with, and has impregnated, his close friend's wife. Many of the players in the 1950s Hollywood depicted in *Hail, Caesar!* must hide the fact that they are Communists, or gay, or in various other ways unsavory and disreputable by the standards of the time. And think again of Carl Showalter hiding that money in the snow, trying to make it visible to himself but invisible to everyone else.

Every technology of representation has its own biases toward visibility and invisibility, its own tendencies to bring certain aspects of our experience to light while ignoring or suppressing others. The giddy, buoyant energy of 2016's *Hail, Caesar!* is largely derived from the tension between depth and surface, between presence and absence, as the film cuts between gloriously colorful excerpts from entirely fictional feature films and behind-the-scenes tales of industry scandal and studio shenanigans. The protagonist, Eddie Mannix, is a man whose very job is to make things invisible: he's what is known in Hollywood as a "fixer," someone whose role is to cover up gossip and salacious stories regarding their stars: unsanctioned pregnancies, unacknowledged homosexuality, leftist politics, that sort of thing. To replace those unpalatable stories with more tolerable tales. Thus, the movie studios, frequently portrayed—especially in their own products— as originators of stories, are here acknowledged to be equally interested in suppressing stories. We tell ourselves stories to keep other stories from being told. In *Hail, Caesar!*, those other stories include political ideas that fall outside those tolerated within the American mainstream, represented, here, by a group of Communist screenwriters who are planning a rendezvous with a Soviet submarine. That sleek gray sub is both photogenic and gloriously silly, but it's also a metaphor for everything that, in *Hail, Caesar!*, is concealed under the surface and only rarely comes to light—which is to say, the light projected onto movie screens. (In the film's comedic high point, a song and dance number, "No Dames," featuring a bar's worth of sailors, the homoerotic subtext of many actual mid-century Hollywood musicals is permitted to rise to the surface, with hilarious results.) The Coens pull a clever sleight-of-hand here, presenting Mannix as admirable and sympathetic—indeed, as a kind of Christ figure—while clearly inviting us, beneath the surface, to morally deplore such behaviors, as if the only way Hollywood would even permit this story of capitalist exploitation to be told was by re-envisioning the plot, and the whole moral universe, to make Mannix the hero of the story. As if, in other words, there were a meta-fixer standing behind the story of Eddie the Fixer. "Stories end and stories begin," the narrator sums things up, "but the story of Eddie Mannix will never end." Indeed. For there will always be inconvenient truths to be covered up, and counter-mainstream ideas to be silenced. The work of the fixers is never done.

The idea that a movie screen is anything but a direct, transparent, and innocent portal to reality pervades the Coens' films, but *Hail, Caesar!*, by taking filmmaking as its very subject, lays it before us with a new and biting ferocity. In the film that followed, *The Ballad of Buster Scruggs*, the Coens again laid their cards on the table while returning to the Western genre, this time focusing their, and our, attention on storytelling itself. An anthology of six tales set, once again, squarely in the Western mode, the film is presented as a set of stories, organized by the graphic of a leatherbound book that flips pages between segments, each of which presents yet another chapter of the America frontier adventure. These adventures, almost without exception, end in death; but what is most notable is the number of characters who are led to their deaths by their naïve and trusting faith in stories. In the title story, the singing cowboy Buster Scruggs has cast himself in the lead role of a quasi-religious myth that leads inevitably to his own death at the hands of a younger, faster gunslinger with an even sweeter singing voice. Alice Longabaugh, the title character of "The Gal Who Got Rattled," dies by her own hand, having been convinced by a story about the savagery of the Sioux that suicide was a preferable fate. (Ironically, she is the person to whom Billy Knapp had remarked that an attitude of uncertainty is "appropriate for the matters of this world." Like so many Coen characters, she failed

64

to pay enough attention to the proffered lesson.) In the concluding segment, "The Mortal Remains"—a delightfully macabre mix of John Ford, Ambrose Bierce, and Jean-Paul Sartre—the connection between stories and death is made explicit. The segment is set entirely inside a traveling stagecoach. During the journey, two characters, Thigpen and Clarence (and who can doubt that they stand for the Coen brothers themselves?) are revealed to their fellow stagecoach passengers—who, it turns out, are already dead, and on their way to some sort of undetermined afterlife—to be Grim Reapers, emissaries of death. A traveling duo whose primary business is separating people's souls from their bodies, the one keeping the victims entertained, while the other "thumps" the life out of them. "We all love hearing about ourselves," Thigpen tells them, "over and over. So long as the people in the story are—us but not us. Not us at the end, especially. The Midnight Caller gets him, never me. I'll live forever … So I tell the stories, and Clarence thumps. He's *very* good."

Indeed. Stories end and stories begin, but the storytelling—and the thumping—go on forever.

TWO MORE MONTHS

You know—for kids!

Norville Barnes, *The Hudsucker Proxy*

I love him SO MUCH!

—Ed, *Raising Arizona*

What is highly visible in *Fargo*, and yet silenced—almost entirely unspoken, until the very end—is the fact that Chief of Police Marge Gunderson is seven months pregnant. She and her husband, Norm, have made the decision to bring a child into this world. Anything she learns about the world at this point, then—its nature, its inhospitality, the fact that it is a dwelling place for radical evil—will be amplified in its import.

Let me tell you about something that happened to me. In early 2020 I was on a flight from Chicago to California. The coronavirus was just beginning to take over the headlines; a few people, though as yet not many, had uttered the word "pandemic." Like a lot of people, I have not been on an airplane since. As we landed in Sacramento, the passenger next to me took out his phone and reestablished contact with the world. I glanced and saw that he was scrolling through his Facebook feed, which consisted almost entirely of conservative, pro-Republican memes. A picture of Donald Trump, smiling and appearing confident and competent, with the caption: I STILL TRUST THIS MAN. And below it, a photo of Greta Thunberg, accompanied by a mocking caption to the effect that if children want a cleaner planet, they could start by tidying up their rooms.

There are millions of Greta Thunbergs out there. Young children who are going to have to live in the world their parents' and grandparents' generations will leave them. Children who are terrified because they, unlike so many of their elders, are still sufficiently in contact with reality to understand that that world is not what it should be. And who, when faced with these difficult facts, have too much strength, or too much integrity, or simply too much love for the truth, to turn away and take shelter behind a Facebook wall of mocking memes. But then the truth, for these young people, is a matter of life or death.

What stories are their parents telling, about their children, about their own decisions? Imagine being a young person, trying to talk to your parents about the fact that you are frightened that by the time you are their age, there won't be enough arable land or clean drinking water left on the planet to support whatever human population remains. And

66 imagine having your parents smile and say to you, How cute. You want to clean up the planet? Start with your room. Imagine your parents telling you stories about how global warming is only a story, that the real danger is posed by violent immigrants sneaking across the border. Imagine being a student at a school where, one day, without warning, thirty-four of your fellow students are killed or injured by a young man armed with a semi-automatic rifle. This is a true story. I am telling it exactly as it occurred. But now imagine hearing that many people on the internet have been convinced that the incident never happened, that the whole thing had been staged by George Soros, or Antifa, or some other entity that opposed the Second Amendment. No one was actually shot. No one actually had a gun. What? You saw it with your own eyes? The blood? The panicked screams? Think again.

Maybe it was only a movie.

In terms of politics, values, and demographics, the Americans who are most likely to advance or believe such conspiracy theories, or to pass along funny memes mocking Greta Thunberg, are the same ones who have been convinced by news reports that we need to secure our national borders in order to protect our children. They are the same ones most likely to believe stories saying that Covid-19 is a hoax, a pretext for government to remove such critical freedoms as the rights to eat in restaurants and breathe in other people's faces. That senior Democrats and their friends are engaged in a massive program of child abuse and enslavement. That Donald Trump was appointed president by God in order to root out this evil. That Biden stole the election. That the mob that rioted and stormed the Capitol building in early January was composed of American patriots who were merely beginning a revolution that remains to be completed. That this revolution must be completed. For the good of the country.

When I think about these things, I think about the moment in *Fargo* when Stan Grossman reminds Jerry Lundegaard that Jean is not the only victim of the kidnapping: someone is going to have to find a way to reassure Scotty, Jean and Jerry's son. You can see in Jerry's reaction that he has quite literally forgotten that he *has* a son—a real person, a human being who will be affected by his schemes. "Yah, geez. *Scotty.*" As it happens, from *Raising Arizona* through *Hail, Caesar!*, there are more children in Coen films than one at first realizes. Children who are profoundly vulnerable to the thoughtless, selfish, or simply stupid actions of the adults who ought to have been caring for them. Children who are real victims—worthy victims—of the absurd, self-serving stories their parents and other adults are so quick to tell and so eager to believe.

Fargo ends with Marge having returned home to her husband, Norm. Things have come full circle: they lie in bed, in the glow of the TV—for once, we can barely hear it, and it doesn't seem to matter—and talk about little things, literally: the three cent stamp, which Norm's artwork will soon adorn, and which, as Marge reassuringly points out, people still use, when the price of postage goes up and people who still have the old stamps have to make up the difference. (The introduction of the "Forever" stamp, one supposes, was a bad thing for people like Norm.) Then, at last, in the final words of the film, they refer to her pregnancy. "Two more months," he says, gently patting her belly, his face aglow in the comforting radiance of the TV screen. "Two more months," she replies.

It's a sweet, tender moment, and some have chosen to read it as an unambiguously happy ending. But the look on Marge's face when she utters the film's final line contains as much apprehension as it does joyful anticipation. And as viewers, we know more than Norm about what Marge has just been through, what she has learned about the world they are bringing this child into, and what she has seen, even if she chooses to keep it invisible and silent in that cozy domestic space.

68 She knows what is waiting outside, out there in the cold; she knows, now, what the walls of their modest but comfortable house were erected to shelter them from, to prevent from entering. She knows what is out there in the snow, the snow that is always, it seems, gently falling in that part of the world. The snow that will cover up any sign we might make, that will silence any word we might say, fix any story we might tell, concealing our actions, evil and good, under a blanket of blankness. The snow keeps falling, it never really stops, and in the end it covers us all. True story. 🙢

Troy Jollimore is Professor of Philosophy at California State University, Chico. A former recipient of a National Book Critics Circle Award for poetry and a Guggenheim Fellowship, he is the author of three books of philosophy and four books of poetry, including the forthcoming Earthly Delights.

FRIEND

DOMINICA PHETTEPLACE

She says Namaste even when not in yoga class, whereas I will not say om under any circumstances.

She says she doesn't resent the younger generation, that they are completely of a world that we made, that to hate the young is to hate ourselves.

She says that guys on dating apps indicate their marriage suitability by listing their hobbies as 'hiking' and 'rock climbing.'

Her hobbies include cocaine and gambling, but she leaves those off her profile.

Somedays she doesn't feel like getting out of bed, but if I say I want to get coffee she will walk with me down the avenue to the best café, the one that hasn't yet been ruined by Instagram.

It'll all work out, she says, and I agree even though I don't.

Plan A is being admired by the world for your intellect and walking the path of your true calling but until then we have each other.

✿

Later in the day, I text her:

Let's go to Japan

I want the $22 fruit plate in Sembikaya, the one that comes with half
a banana and three peeled grapes

                                                  or let's go to Paris

and bathe in a Dirand tub made of a single piece of marble.

She writes back:

> No more stories about being a tourist in another country, please,
> and none about funerals or affairs,
>
> no miscarriages or cancer or things lost in a fire.
>
> Just write about what's good and what feels good and help me
> too because
>
> I am not good at titles or tweets, all of my poems are twenty
> pages long
>
> and I cry even when I get personal rejections
>
> tell me they aren't worth it

✿

She wants a ripped T-shirt, but she doesn't want to cut the material
herself, won't even watch a video tutorial on how to be artfully
distressed.

I tell her that virtue signaling is for Libras even as I pine for a Libra.
In my next career I will be an astrologer and then I will know what
kind of Libras to avoid.

Plan A is to face the sunrise bravely but until then we will fave each
other's tweets while we squint at the horizon.

AFTER

DOMINICA PHETTEPLACE

After the singularity, it made sense to start over on a new social
network, one where there were no pictures of me.
Ignore the people who are wrong and don't know it yet and the
internet is reduced to a minefield of crushes and ways to get crushed.
I resolved to stop stalking my rivals, to quit haunting their feeds like
an insatiable ghost, but in order to follow through I needed:
a thousand loyal followers and a selfie that could purify my soul.
Then I remembered an important email I received years ago and
never responded to.
Then the times I didn't say thank you and should have.
From now on, I will tell people I like them, instead of silently keeping
them as open tabs in my heart.

Dominica Phetteplace is a writer and futurist. She is the recipient of a Pushcart Prize and a Rona Jaffe Award. Her work has appeared in Asimov's, Catapult, Analog, and other publications.

THE SINS OF OTHERS

HÉCTOR TOBAR

Juan H. woke up one Saturday morning with two strange men standing over his bed. One was wearing a loose-fitting navy-colored vest labelled ICE; his purpose was clear enough. But the other guy was in jeans smudged with grease stains. A working man, "Karl," according to the oval patch on his shirt. There was something disheveled about both of them. As if they, and not him, had just been roused from their slumbers.

The agent held a piece of paper before Juan, and gestured for him to stand up. When Juan moved to take the paper, the agent pulled it back.

"I'd like to be out of here by 7:30, if you don't mind," the agent said.

The agent was a lean man with the gray and brittle sheen of a lifelong smoker, and a nicotine patch on his neck. He looked around the room, and the orderliness he saw seemed to unsettle him: a hardwood floor, and pictures of Juan and his family members on a dresser, a humidifier, purring steadily, and nothing else. There was something spartan, or Scandinavian about the space. Not a single article of clothing was tossed about.

"You think this is easy for me?" the agent said. "I've got a wife and kid. They see me leave with my gun, my taser, my handcuffs at five in the morning. They wonder what their father does."

Juan climbed out of bed, and as he did so the officer approached,

took him by the arm, turned him so that he was facing Karl, and prepared   73
to wrap plastic ties around Juan's wrists.

"Can I get dressed first?" Juan asked.

"Yeah, go ahead." The officer watched Juan take some pants and a shirt from his dresser and said, "We feel terrible about what Karl did."

"I do too," Karl said.

"But the law's the law."

Juan considered himself an informed person. He had read stories about the Replacement Law. But up to this moment they were like folktales, or dispatches from another country, because the substance of the Replacement Law was strange, mean and, in its own way, childish.

His adult daughter squeezed into the room now, past a second agent Juan could see in the hallway outside. She took in the tableau before her: the agent, her father in handcuffs, Karl.

"What's going on?" she demanded.

"He drank too much, he hit a pedestrian," the officer said, pointing with the warrant at Karl. "The pedestrian happens to be Karl's wife. She's got two broken vertebrae. That's no picnic. Do you have two broken vertebrae, Juan? No, you don't. So consider yourself lucky. You're a lucky man today."

"I feel terrible," Karl said.

"Do you know this man, Papá," Juan's daughter asked, pointing at Karl.

After the three minutes Karl had been in Juan's bedroom, Juan finally recognized him. "He used to work at the shop," Juan said. "Hace muchos años."

"But Juan here isn't so innocent either, is he?" the agent said, pointing with the piece of paper at Juan.

"What is he charged with?" Juan's daughter asked.

"Your father isn't charged with anything. Karl is the one who's charged. What I'm saying is that Juan here is no white swan. True, he didn't commit an attempted homicide against his wife with a Ford F-150 truck: Karl did that. But he is who he is." The officer took a moment to peruse the document in his hand. "I'm referring, specifically, to the events of September, 1996."

"Oh, I see," Juan H. said.

"What? Crossing the border? But that was twenty-four years ago," Juan's daughter said. "Before I was born." She spoke these last words to the backs of her father, the agent, and Karl as they filed out the bedroom door.

The agent led Juan out of his house and into a small, concrete front yard, past the triple-level concrete fountain Juan had installed there, and past the shrine to the Virgin his late wife had asked him to build. The agent saw a switch on a pole next to the Virgin, and he flipped it on, and a string of light bulbs came on around the Virgin and the concrete aureole that enveloped her. The lights flashed yellow, and then red, and the Virgin's eyes gleamed with these colors, and then with blue, orange, and magenta. "That's pretty cool," he said.

The agent opened the gate, and led Juan to a large, unmarked Chevrolet Suburban, where two other agents were waiting, and smoking cigarettes, which they extinguished when they saw the agent wearing the nicotine patch.

Karl walked away, alone, advancing down the sidewalk, and used a remote key to unlock the doors of a Ford F-150 truck which was double-parked nearby; it gleamed with a freshly polished skin that reflected Karl's body like a mirror of undulating obsidian. One of the agents followed after him, and shook Karl's hand; then he patted him on the back.

"You picked a good one," the agent said. "I think this guy is going to stick."

Just before the agents lowered Juan's head and guided him into the Suburban, Karl turned to look at Juan one last time. The Mexican mechanic was dressed in green corduroy pants and a T-shirt for the University of Oregon (his oldest son's alma mater), and his expression was one of annoyance and resignation. A good man who accepts a fate he does not deserve. Karl admired him as one does a spiffy prom date, or a tall, lean, and especially fast horse.

✳   ✳   ✳

After an hour in the normal, awful traffic of the city, the Suburban entered a large parking lot surrounded by fences, driving past the soiled pink cubes of an abandoned shopping center, to a building that stood like an island in the center of an asphalt sea. They stopped before the building's breezeblock facade; on either side of the front doors, there was a cluster of bird of paradise plants with frayed leaves.

The agents guided Juan through a pair of glass doors, into a room marked Reception, and he saw a desk, behind which there were many small squares with hooks, some of which held keys, and a large sign that read Quality Inn. From a bag marked Housekeeping, the agents removed a set of pale-yellow overalls, and gave them to him.

"Go change in the bathroom," one of the agents said while removing Juan's hand-ties. When he returned from the bathroom, the agents had Juan sign many forms. They told him to stand in front of a white sheet hung up next to an empty fish tank that smelled of algae and grime, and they snapped his photograph.

One of the agents handed him a key attached to a plastic oval imprinted with the number 206. Then the agent joined the others, who were leaving the lobby, and Juan watched as they locked the glass doors, and drove away in the Suburban.

How long would he be here? Was there nothing he could do to appeal his detention? The agents had disappeared before Juan could ask them the many questions he had, and he was left alone to contemplate his situation. Pulled out of his bed, to be punished for a crime committed by Karl. You hear about these happenings on the radio, in the news on your phone, but they seem far away from you, and then you are inside the machinery, and it processes you, and there is nothing you can do.

When he found Room 206 and unlocked the door, Juan entered a carpeted room that held two sets of bunk beds with three snoring men. He took an empty, bottom bunk, and sat on the edge. As he waited for the other men to wake up, he studied the two paintings on the walls. One depicted a lake with lily pads. Or maybe it was a swamp, because a fetid yellow mist seemed to be drifting over the water. No, it was just dust on the painting's surface. In the second painting, two deer with bodies disproportionate to their legs stood in a forest of birch trees; they turned to face the viewer with a kind of disdain, like haughty, furry, four-legged fashion models.

✳   ✳   ✳

When his new roommates woke up, they introduced themselves. He told them he worked as a car mechanic, and described the agent's sudden appearance in his home with Karl. And they, in turn, shared the stories of the people whose misdeeds had brought them to this place.

"My guy robbed a liquor store," Pedro X. said.

"El mío sold some of that crystal drug," said Oscar J. "To a police officer! ¡Pendejo!"

"Mine set fire to his old elementary school," said Joaquín Z. "He's nineteen. A real mocoso. Lo extraño is that I sort of like him. He reminds me of me, when I was back at the Prepa in el DF. I did all sorts of crazy things." Joaquín Z. stared out the window, lost in memories for a moment. "But never with fire," he said finally, with a distant voice.

"That's going too far."

"The Replacement Law is ridiculous," Juan said, and he began to rail to his roommates about the cruelty of that piece of legislation, and the idiocy of the elected officials who had approved it. As he spoke, he felt reason and logic alive within him, the nobility of the lessons about democracy he'd learned in grade school in his native country.

"You talk really well for a car mechanic," Joaquin Z. said. "And you're right. This is totally fucked." And then Joaquin Z. threw himself back on his bed, and everyone was silent, and nothing more was said about the subject.

A day passed. And then another. Every morning at 9:30 the inmates left their room and walked down to a breakfast buffet in an old conference room, joining about fifty others in scooping up runny scrambled eggs and discs of reconstituted fried potatoes onto their plates. When they weren't eating, the inmates filled their days sitting in the big courtyard of the building, which was surrounded on four sides by two stories of rooms. They slumped and lounged on plastic chairs by a waterless swimming pool, each man dressed, like Juan, in a yellow jumpsuit with the words DETENTION KINGS, INC., stenciled across the back. Joaquin Z., a small and funny man, liked to climb into the empty pool and sit at the bottom, cross-legged, meditating. He said sounds gathered there, and that he could hear the conversations of the people who were in the parking lot, outside, and passing trains, and birds singing from miles away.

Juan walked through the hallways, making circles around the facility, and once he found his way back to the lobby, and to a side room that was completely empty, expect for a display of brochures and flyers. "Wine Tasting Tour!" promised one pamphlet. "Whitewater Aquatics Park!" announced another. Juan took a brochure for the museum to the local historical society, and opened it, and as he walked back to Room 206 he read about old silver mines and "frontier Ghost towns" and "Old West cemeteries" and "free samples of homemade ice cream made by our past president, Clarissa Johnson."

✳ ✳ ✳

On Juan H.'s fourth day in detention, a group of agents arrived and fanned out through the facility, knocking on doors and calling out names. The agent with the nicotine patch entered Room 206 and found Juan.

"Today you get to see a judge," the agent explained. "Habeas corpus."

Juan followed him and a group of other agents and inmates, down the building's concrete stairs, back to the lobby, and then out the glass doors to the parking lot, where a fleet of Suburbans waited, each humming and emitting aromas of carbon monoxide and heated plastic.

The agents gestured for Juan to take a seat, and he did so, grateful that they did not handcuff him. Soon the caravan of Suburbans pushed forward through the normal, awful traffic of the city.

The Suburbans stopped before an office building in the city center. Across the street, there was a pleasant park, with trees and people walking dogs and old men rolling bocce balls on a lawn. With his agent guiding him by the arm, Juan entered the building via the front steps and when they walked into the lobby, Juan saw men carrying briefcases, and a delivery man holding flowers, and he caught a glimpse of the building directory, which listed insurance companies, marketing consultants, and doctors' offices.

Juan and his agent entered an elevator, stepping in behind another inmate in a yellow jumpsuit marked DETENTION KINGS INC., and an inmate whose avocado green jumpsuit was stamped with the words HENDERSON BROS. DETENTION CORP. When the elevator reached the tenth floor, the agent led Juan out.

"Go to Suite 1016," the agent said. "Wait for me there. I gotta take a leak."

Juan H. walked down the hallway, searching for Suite 1016, and he found it, and a sign with the words Immigration Court. But he did not go inside. After a few steps more he found a door marked Stairs, and opened it, and looked down. A breeze flowed upward through the stairwell, a taste of the open air and freedom awaiting him.

Before Juan could take his first, liberated step he imagined a life of moving from one place to the next, hiding. But if he stayed and faced the judge, maybe he could persuade the court to set him free. He imagined the judge as a sage older gentleman. A man in a bow tie, with glasses. He would tell the judge: I don't deserve to be punished in this way. I've lived my life well. They need me at the shop, especially to work on those new electric vehicles that come in from time to time, which no one else wants to touch. And except for the events of September 1996, I'm not guilty of anything; and even that one thing wasn't a crime, in a moral and human sense, because I was just trying to provide for my family. Juan H. thought of his home and its daily rhythms; his daughter out the door, heading off to her college classes; his son off to work, always punctual. The sunlit warmth of his home when his wife was still alive and their son and daughter were small children. She forgave me everything before she went. Everything.

Juan H. had allowed the door to the stairwell to close, and was standing before it, as if in a trance, when he heard a voice behind him. "Suite 1016 is this way." Juan turned and saw the agent. "This way, buddy," the agent said.

In Suite 1016 Juan saw a series of walnut benches squeezed into a space the size of a three-car garage. When he sat down, Juan noticed the kneelers: the benches were old church pews. They faced a small steel desk on a riser, with two nameplates; one stamped in plastic that read "Judge Pro Tempore" and another that was written on paper with

80   a Sharpie: Caitlyn "Kate" Alford, Esq. The judge was a woman in her mid- to late-twenties, Juan guessed, and was dressed not in a robe, but in a stylishly cut, double-breasted, light gray blazer.

The judge had three stacks of files on her desk, and now she took one, and reading the file tab, called out, "Segerstrom!" The agent took Juan by his elbow, and gestured for him to stand. "We're here," the agent said.

"The defendant, Karl Segerstrom, is eligible for bail," the judge said. "In light of the circumstances, which, I see, include a statement from the alleged victim, in which she states, 'I wish to drop the charges, I love his stupid ass,' I'm going to order the defendant's release. Forthwith."

From the front row of benches, the voice of an unseen male called out: "The government chooses to appeal, your honor."

The agent stood up, walked up to the judge's desk, and took a thick file folder that was handed to him.

"Upstairs," the agent said to Juan. "Suite 1224. Let's go."

They took the elevator up to the twelfth floor. When they reached Suite 1224, the agent stopped before a sign that read: Iris Cruz, DDS, Periodontist.

"Aw shit, I mixed up the number again," the agent said. "It's 1242, not 1224. Fucking dyslexia."

They found Suite 1242, and entered a small waiting room, where magazines and medical brochures were stacked haphazardly including one with a cartoon of a tooth with a face that was pouting and crying. "Your root canal and you," it said. A sign warned Medical Gasses, No Smoking. The agent reached through a sliding glass window, and handed the Segerstrom file to a woman who sat behind a desk. She wore a blue, floral print smock, with a badge that read Appeals Express, LLP.

"Do we go in to see the judge?" Juan H. asked.

"We don't see the appeals judge. No," the agent said. "He's back there, somewhere. Or she is. They are."

Fifteen minutes later, the woman behind the glass announced: "Segerstrom!" The agent stood up. "That's my guy. Whattaya got for me?"

"The appeal's been granted," the woman said. "Your detainee stays in custody."

"Got it," the agent said, and he turned to Juan and gestured for him to get up, and the two men walked out the door and down the hall to wait for the elevator.

❋   ❋   ❋

They drove back to the detention center, arriving just before sunset, the breezeblock facade bathed in orange light. Juan H. returned to Room 206, and found his roommates there, and each looked up at him with a kind of weariness, or recognition, and said nothing.

Two weeks passed, and Juan did not hear another word about his case. He found no official he could complain to; the agents were present only when they delivered new inmates, and to take them to hearings at immigration court. The staff of the detention center consisted of cooks, and a small janitorial staff, but no one with any true authority. The phones Juan found (including one underneath his bunk) played bossa nova music when he picked them up, and did not work for making calls.

One day, Juan took a circular walk around the compound, and on his fifth lap he took a right down a dimly lit, apparently abandoned corridor on the ground floor, and arrived at a door that was marked with red letters, "EMERGENCY EXIT. DO NOT OPEN. ALARM WILL SOUND." He pushed it open, but there was no alarm, just the sound of traffic entering the corridor. The bright light and asphalt plain of an empty parking lot stretched before him, and in the distance he saw the silhouette of a freeway, and a thoroughfare with cars speeding past.

Juan stepped out, and he heard and felt the door closing behind

82 him, and he walked at an unhurried pace away from the detention center. When he reached the thoroughfare he headed west, in the general direction of his home. He walked one mile, then two, passing industrial parks, golf courses, and car dealerships, and all these places felt dry and dusty, and the few people he saw were mute and did not look at him, despite the yellow jumpsuit he was wearing.

After two hours of walking, Juan H. entered a residential neighborhood of small homes with humble yards and slanted roofs that were worn and patched. He saw a vendor in a straw hat, standing before a cart beneath a traffic light.

"Elotes! Elotes!" the vendor called out. Juan was hungry. "Tengo hambre, pero no tengo dinero," he said to the vendor, who was a short and very young man. The vendor looked at Juan, and the yellow overalls he was wearing, and gave a nod of understanding. He took two corn cobs from his cart, and wrapped them in paper, and gave them to Juan, who said gracias. Juan H. ate as he continued his march westward, and ten minutes later he reached a bus stop and saw a sign that named a destination that was close to his home. Two women were waiting on a bench. Juan took a seat next to them and said, "No tengo dinero para la feria," addressing no one in particular; it was a spoken thought, a lament. One of the women reached into the pocket of her apron, and she produced two bills, and handed them to him. Then she placed a hand on his wrist and said, "Que Dios te proteja." The bus arrived, and Juan H. got on, and for two hours the bus plowed forward, through the normal, awful traffic of the city, until it reached the end of its route, and Juan began to walk the final two miles home.

Juan arrived home at dusk, and his adult daughter and son watched him enter the house, emerging from a gray-blue half-light, and for a moment he looked like a hologram of the man they knew as their father. But when they saw him in the amber, incandescent light inside their living room, he came to life in all his true textures: Juan Ignacio Hernández Pérez, age forty-six, car mechanic and amateur philosopher. Looking very tired and diminished in stature, somehow, by the yellow overalls he was wearing.

✽ ✽ ✽

In the days that followed, Juan tended the backyard garden his wife had started in the final year of her life. He went to the auto shop and his boss said, "Glad to have you back." No one mentioned his absence, or his detention, except for the time he was on his back underneath a BMW, and one of his co-workers said, sotto voce, "When they get you for that, it's like a black hole. Happened to my cousin. Haven't seen him in a year. I thought we might never see you again."

Finally, a letter from the government arrived in the mail. "Your release was approved," said the letter inside; it was dated five days after his escape from the detention center. "Your continued parole from detention is conditional on the good behavior of The Accused."

When Juan went to bed at night, he thought of Karl Segerstrom, and this caused him trouble sleeping. So he purchased a machine that made ocean noises, and the electric waves crashing on an electric beach soothed him, and soon he was having a pleasant, recurring dream that unfolded in the scrublands of his youth, and on plains of agave and cornfields. He saw the form of his wife's body, walking ahead of him, but never glimpsed her face, and when he woke up he felt a fleeting sense of joy, and then a deep and enduring sense of loss.

Six months passed in this way.

Then one morning Juan opened his eyes to the sound of waves crashing on a beach, and the gray eyes of the agent with the nicotine patch, and the face of Karl Segerstrom, which was covered in bruises and cuts.

"Karl found the guy who was banging his old lady," the agent said. "Tried to mess him up. It sorta backfired on Karl, as you can see. Aggravated assault is the charge this time."

"I'm going to find that peckerwood," Karl said, "and I'm going kill him."

"Now, now, Karl. Don't say that. You're scaring Juan here. Murder in the first: that's a life sentence, boy."

And soon Juan H. was returning to the detention center in a Suburban that rumbled eastward, away from his home, surging and slowing and stopping and surging through the normal, awful traffic of the city.

✻   ✻   ✻

Juan H. entered Room 206 and saw the familiar faces of Pedro X., Oscar J., and Joaquín Z., and the painting of the swamp and the deer that loomed over the room, and the phone on the floor that played bossa nova music.

"Hola," Joaquín Z. said, and the other two roommates made noises that may have been words, or may not have been.

Many days and months passed. When Juan wandered down to the darkened corridor with the emergency exit, he found the door locked. Winter came, and the days turned shorter, and when it rained the inmates turned to playing card games inside the breakfast room, and then spring came, and they returned to the courtyard.

Finally, one morning, Juan heard a knock at the door to Room 206. He rose to his feet, and opened the door, and saw the agent who had worn the nicotine patch—only now the patch was gone, and the agent smelled of cigarette smoke. The agent handed him a blue slip of paper. It was a color copy of an official document, a "Certificate of Death." Juan studied the form, afraid he might see the name of one of his children. Or perhaps the name of Karl's murder victim. Instead, he read: Decedent: Karl Ulysses Segerstrom. Cause Of Death: Suicide.

"Karl's old lady finally told him to fuck off," the agent said. "She filed for divorce. So Karl shot himself. With a shotgun. Ugly way to go. Super messy."

Juan tried to hand the document back to the agent.

"Keep it," the agent said. "You may need it one day. You never know when the government might lose something, get something mixed up. Always keep your paperwork."

Juan followed the agent back down to the lobby. Another agent handed him the bag in which Juan had deposited his street clothes many months earlier. The agent who no longer wore a nicotine patch said: "Go to the bathroom and change."

When Juan was done dressing, he returned to the lobby and saw the agents driving away in a Suburban, the unlocked glass doors behind them still moving in their wake. He walked out the door, and retrieved the wallet and the phone that he'd left in his pants pocket months earlier. He turned on the phone: To his surprise, it worked. He called his daughter, and asked her to come and pick him up, and for the next hour he waited for her, sitting by the dust-covered bird of paradise plants, listening to the traffic passing on the nearby thoroughfare. He wondered how many years the shopping center next door had been closed.

✳ ✳ ✳

After work, and on the weekends, Juan took long walks through his neighborhood. When he encountered a man or woman living a desperate and frayed existence, he studied them. There were many such individuals in his neighborhood, and each time Juan imagined this person committing a crime. A stabbing, a robbery, shoplifting. He caught glimpses of graffiti written on the sidewalk, and he worried about the people who had committed these acts of vandalism. One

86 graffito was repeated again and again, inch-high letters written with a paint-pen scrawl on the iron covers to city water valves: Weedwolf. The Weedwolf probably lived in this neighborhood, and he might know Juan, or know of him. People talked about Juan H.'s case, he sensed this. For decades he'd belonged to the category "Unauthorized Alien," and now his neighbors knew the government had classified him into the subcategory "Nominated Alien Inmate Second." Each time he took a walk, he saw the name Weedwolf, and after a while he imagined the Weedwolf as a bearded man of about his own age, a trickster with ivory teeth, a man who didn't give a shit. He felt the eyes of the Weedwolf gazing upon him, surreptitiously. The tortured, slanted writing of the graffito suggested mental illness, and Juan wondered how much longer would pass before the police arrested Weedwolf and chose Juan to serve his detention.

Juan began to take longer walks, to escape the streets that had been defaced by the Weedwolf, and at the end of one such stroll he entered an unfamiliar neighborhood and saw a storefront with a window advertising weapons. Columbia Firearms.

Juan thought that if the agent came for him again, he would find a way to escape detention and return to this place, to purchase a gun. Then he would track down the Weedwolf. But Juan was uncertain whether he would have the courage for what needed to happen next. ✂

Héctor Tobar is the author of the novels The Tattooed Soldier, The Barbarian Nurseries, *and most recently,* The Last Great Road Bum (MCD / Farrar, Straus & Giroux).

TAKE CARE OF ME ON THE EARTH

CHRIS CAROSI

Take care of me on the earth, not in computer-hand. Take care of me like the plug of light anyone eats. Take a sworn body to a sworn road. Swear on the steep road. Lost a lawnmower down there by Highland Middle School. Gave up like I gave up filling a machine with gas. Walked. I pushed through a thorny bush, in the clearing a pheasant scared the shit out of me. My dad taught me how to shit in the woods. Part of the understanding was there was never any understanding between us. That we barked on the driveway like old cars. We sat among each other like earwigs and wiffle-ball bats. The shed was my military base, and it was right here where I lay on the ramp where we drove the lawnmower up and cried. Full view of me from the large kitchen window. It's a rapture of decision that I bawled. Weak like a backyard is weak. What mattered was that I could surrender at any time to this, clean. I was the most mature little kid because I could say to you without blinking that I hated it and loved it every day.

Chris Carosi is the author of the poetry chapbooks Funerals and Others (Inverted Church), bright veil, and FICTIONS. "Take Care of Me on the Earth" is from a recently completed manuscript of poems.

COLLAPSE

AMANDA MOORE

What do bees want? is a question I've never asked
myself or any expert. I know they need

to gather pollen & nectar, need water & shelter,
though they can make their own of any hollow place.

But as to *want*, who can say? I say
I need to take my vitamins, apply sunscreen,

eat greens and exercise—want self-care, something
I deserve (for what I do not know).

Our bodies are built to decay. I opened
the hive only as often as I was told:

to check brood, the health of the queen.
I did not know what I was looking for but trusted

diligence would keep us from disaster.
They wanted me out of their way,

and so I closed it all up,
left them to their desires.

Amanda Moore's first collection of poetry, Requeening, *was selected for the 2020 National Poetry Series by Ocean Vuong and is forthcoming from Ecco in October.*

BIODOME

JUHEA KIM

April 13. Almost midnight. Through the worn twill curtains, a viscous light was flowing into the apartment like amber. Park washed his face in the bathroom, took his meds, and sat down on the sofa with the remote. One click, and the blue light of the TV mingled with the sodium yellow of the room. He flipped through the channels. Game shows. Contestants competing for money, for marriage. The women are showing off, swiveling their hips and winking at the camera, and then they're ranked by the amount of applause they receive. People awwing over tiny puppies. Slow, close-up shots of some new hybrid food, a rare delicacy. A man has to eat a glistening pile of meat and cheese until his face is streaming with sweat and an exhausted howl escapes from his mouth. Woops, applause, groans, laughter.

A pair of professors seated facing one another against a black backdrop. No audience, no clapping.

"There are generations of children who are growing up not knowing the meaning of the word 'rain,' 'snow,' 'clouds,' who have never seen the sea or the sunset in their lives. Are you saying that this is not a moral crisis?" said the pundit on the right side, a literature professor at Seoul National University.

"You are making a Romanticist error in conflating nature with morality. Nature in itself is neither good nor evil. Likewise, technology

90 that is used to shape or control nature is neither inherently moral nor immoral. Less than two centuries ago, our ancestors argued over the morality of the 'Iron Horse.' Would you argue that the subway is evil because it bores through the earth and shuttles around humans in a sealed underground passageway?" said the pundit on the left side, a philosophy professor at Korea University. "Technology is strictly a matter of utility, not ethics."

"I would be greatly presumptuous if I were single-handedly conflating nature and morality, as you put it. But take this for an example: You know that language shapes thoughts, ideas, and morals. Even you must acknowledge that in our Korean language, the word 'God' is literally, 'Dear Sky.' Long before I had ever romanticized nature, as you argue, our people have used words of nature to describe what is good and sacred, for five thousand years. When the people no longer know what a sky actually is—and many of the younger generations have never seen it—how would they have any consciousness of a God?"

"You have a false understanding of the nature of faith. God—at least in the Christian sense—defies representation or proof. If one needed the sky in order to recognize God, then that would not be genuine faith at all," the philosophy professor said smugly, then carefully delivered the ultimate insult. "You speak out of sentimentality."

"I'm not being sentimental. I'm being human," his opponent replied calmly.

And on and on they went. Park turned off the TV.

"This is a nice place," Park said. They were seated in the courtyard garden of an elegant restaurant in Gangnam, surrounded by trellises and arbors of roses, jasmine, and other dark and lush shrubs that Park didn't recognize. The waiters in waistcoats flitted about discreetly like moths, lighting candles one by one.

"How many of these have you done?" Jina asked.

"What?"

"You know, *mat sun*."

"Excuse me?"

"You are thirty-five and unmarried so you must have gone on at least two dozen."

"What else do you know about me?"

"The matchmaker gave me the usual specs. Your height, your looks. You're a senior engineer at the Department of Environmental Protection and you graduated from Seoul National University near the top of your class. But you don't have much family money or the ability to finance a new apartment for us. You're the only son of a widowed mother, which is guaranteed to scare off squeamish women. Physically, you have weak lungs, a common enough condition for those born before the Bio. However, I heard you have an IQ in the top 0.1%. So naturally, we may be a match."

"You certainly speak your mind, don't you."

"Here's what I think. I'm twenty-eight and the last of three daughters, so my parents are absolutely dying to get rid of me. My two older sisters both married at twenty-six although I'm much prettier and more intelligent than they are. My parents think it's because of my personality. I don't care much about shutting my mouth to flatter some man who is more stupid than I am. Do you care if I smoke?" She said, already reaching for her cigarette case.

"Be my guest."

"I'm terribly bored by my parents' endless entreaties and machinations. I'm just ready to end it all and marry whomever they think is appropriate. I'm tired. Do you know what I mean?"

"I think I do."

She smiled.

"You know, it's funny. I feel like I can be honest with you. It's not often that I feel that way at one of these things. The matchmaker did say we were an uncommonly good match with our astrological signs."

"Western or traditional?"

She raised an eyebrow.

"Why, traditional of course. Why would I put any trust in Western astrology for something as important as marriage? That stuff is just a bunch of nonsense."

"They seem about equal in my esteem," Park said.

She broke into a peal of silvery laughter. "I'm pleased that you disagree with me. At first I was worried that you'd be one of those scrawny, weak engineer types who don't seem to have any opinions of their own. And please don't take this the wrong way, but your first impression wasn't too far from my expectation. But you know how to push back—I like that." She took a long drag from her cigarette. "I feel like we're going to get along quite well."

Park wished he could come up with some sarcastic remark, but he couldn't. As for himself, he did not yet know whether he liked or disliked Jina. She had a pale heart-shaped face and long, shiny hair falling half way down her back. She was wearing a silk sheath in canary yellow that complemented her ivory skin and jet-black hair. By focusing his eyes on her bare arms, he could almost smell the perfume on her wrists and elbows—floral and slightly musky. Yes, he supposed she was a beautiful woman. He just wasn't sure if he could ever have any feelings for her.

"You look very nice," Park said, at last. Jina's eyes started dancing; she was used to compliments and had been on the verge of impatience with him.

"Nice?" she purred.

"Your dress. It looks beautiful." Park rambled a bit in his embarrassment.

"Oh yes, I suppose. It's yellow so I figured I'd wear it. I see you're not wearing anything for Yellow Day. You don't have a tie or something?"

Park didn't have a yellow tie or socks or anything like that. All day at work, colleagues had teased him about not being in spirit. "Being a spoilsport, Manager Park? Surely you don't want bad luck in the next year?" One of the men, a junior engineer, even jokingly offered to trade a sock with him, so they could each have one that was yellow. But grateful though he was for their good-natured banter, Park was secretly glad about not participating in the whole thing.

"I don't really believe in that stuff," Park said.

"Goodness, you don't believe in anything. Not astrology, not Yellow Day…" Jina smiled. "Is there anything you do believe in?"

Indeed, what did he believe in? He did not know. He was only ever sure about what he couldn't believe in.

The morning after Yellow Day, New Seoul was cast in sepia as usual. There was once a time when trees turned gold in September and October, or so Park was taught in biology class; but the leaves in those photographs were nothing like the color of light here, which was a muggy reddish-brown. Instead of fall leaves, Yellow Day commemorated the Yellow Sand that blew in from the deserts of China and Mongolia each spring, carried by the west wind. This was a phenomenon that was documented in the earliest annals in ancient Korean history, going back at least two millennia. Through most of the twentieth century, the sandstorm happened three days a year in April, leaving a thick layer of dust over everything in the whole country, city and countryside alike. But as the desert in China grew larger, the sandstorm lasted longer: seven days, then twelve, twenty-five, forty-three, sixty-seven. Every consecutive year, the west wind carried even more sand over the Yellow Sea. By the time Park was born, it was calculated that the sand dumped over the Korean peninsula was 1 million tons a year—enough to fill 66,667 dump trucks.

94   One of the earliest consequences of the Yellow Storm was that there was no longer any spring. No more flowers or sitting outside on a park bench, dazed by the scent of the sun warming up the grass. During the day, the sky was always dark gray and thick with particles; at night, it glowed an unearthly red. People couldn't go outside during the Yellow Storm: as soon as you opened the front door, the sand would sting your face like a thousand bees, and swarm into your eyes, nose, and mouth until your lashes crusted over with ash. Even after the storm receded, the toxic sand laced with heavy metals and pesticides remained in the atmosphere so that every breath one took, inside or outside, could cause disease—asthma, interminable coughs, rashes, cancers, and blindness. The sand mingled with clouds in the atmosphere and came down as acid rain, melting down trees and crops. Food prices, already high, became astronomical. There was nothing left on supermarket shelves, even if you could afford it; and anyone who could afford it left the country. Reservoirs and water supplies were found to be contaminated so that no one could drink or even cook with tap water. The rivers became thick with thousands of dead fish. There were protests demanding government action, and eventually riots—eruptions of chaos so that the scant resources could change hands before disappearing completely.

In New Seoul, the poor were counting every grain of rice before a meal, which started from one hundred and dwindled to just ten pieces for dinner. When that ran out, a family would curl up in bed together holding hands, knowing that they would not wake up.

They were saved at last, and only, by the Biodome—completed on April 14, thirty years ago. The first Yellow Day. When it was built, no one objected to it, saying things like the sanctity of the sky or the humanity of nature. They were all just glad to be alive and to breathe the air without worrying it would cause cancer of the throat or lungs. The Bio (BEE-oh), as it was also called, was a clear enclosure of 50-kilometer diameter over New Seoul, blocking off the Yellow Sand and letting in what remnants of sunlight could penetrate the particles. The Bio's internal atmosphere was always a foggy sepia—not because of the sand passing over the enclosure, but because the combined glare of millions of neon lights reflected back on the inner surface of the Bio as a volcanic red-tinged brown, every day and every night.

Naturally, the Bio also eliminated all other precipitation along with the sand, but they found that stable internal humidity and underground watering systems eliminated any real need for rain. It was truly an engineering feat, the world's first successful habitable indoor enclosure at such a scale. And this turned out to be a case in which the problem also provided the solution: The Bio technology became Korea's most important and lucrative export, so that even while importing nearly all food and other products that they no longer made themselves, the country as a whole became more prosperous than ever.

People soon forgot that they were living under a dome. It wasn't that they forgot that it existed, since the Bio was now their livelihood as well as their lifeline. They just ceased to remember that they were under it. After all, it wasn't visible or tangible for most people living inside, and life was better again. Once something became a part of the environment, people accepted it without question and furthermore, forgot that anything had ever been otherwise. It took about a month for the intractable, but for most it was a matter of a few days before they could no longer abide by even the memory of open space. So it was odd to see the television special the other night, with the two aging intellectuals arguing vociferously against one another. And also rather sad, Park thought, to observe those scrawny and balding professors sitting in their ill-fitting suits, each with a glass of tepid water in front of him, talking about what no one thought about with any seriousness or urgency. It had to have been for Yellow Day, commemorating the completion of the Bio thirty years ago. Why that kind of public debate was even included alongside the usual fluff, cooking shows featuring yellow ingredients, or dating contests, he didn't know.

Park himself thought about the Bio quite a lot, but only at his job: his duty as a Senior Engineer in the Department of Environmental Protection, Office of Human Conservation, the Biodome Management Bureau, called for constant monitoring of the main Bio (now there were four total in Korea, and twelve overseas). He had been five when the Bio was built, so he had no true memories of life before it. Sometimes, though, he thought he could remember being on the beach, the heat and the brightness of the sun on his skin and the cool wind that shook his hair, and the achingly bright blue of the sea. He had had dreams where he felt so sure of the sea breeze caressing his cheek that he woke up laughing. But his mother assured him that he'd never been to the beach at all. By the time he was born, the Yellow Storm forbade all but the most necessary excursions outside. His mother said he had never gone out of the house until after the Bio.

There was no wind inside the Bio, only the mechanical exhale of vast ventilators creating corridors of fresh oxygen through the interior smog. So how could he imagine that pressure against his cheeks, the whipping of his hair? How could he imagine something so real if he'd never experienced it? The same way it feels so natural to fly in a dream, Park told himself. After he determined that, he stopped feeling the sea breeze in his sleep. The whole thing put him down with a leaden sense of loss, if it's possible to lose something one has never had.

It was better not to think about the things that weren't here and now, and yet Park had this tendency to drift—and when he consciously stopped himself, he felt caught between two worlds, one occupied by everyone else and the other where he was the sole citizen aside from his strangely companionable thoughts. That latter world wasn't real so he did his best to cling to the first, blending in with the others with his quiet, unassuming demeanor. His unimpressive appearance helped him move along unnoticed: his bony frame with small shoulders, hollow chest, and unobtrusive, mediocre face all gave the impression of a smart though unthreatening engineer-bureaucrat. His teachers had all but pushed him along to become exactly that, praising his even temperament and cognition without rebelliousness. In spite of malnutrition from gestation to age five, the most formative years for his brain, he had excelled in all his exams and personality tests as required. Bio engineering was the most promising field to which all bright students aspired, so he'd applied to that department in the best university in the country and had been accepted. After graduation, he'd applied to just one job at the Department of Environmental Protection, and had stayed there ever since.

In short, the nature of Park's effortless existence was akin to being pushed by the crowd on a packed subway platform. During rush hour, he didn't really walk so much as let himself be picked up and carried by the compressed mass of bodies around him, moving in mindless unity like a school of fish. Getting out at his stop at Yeouido required much more maneuvering, and Park carefully picked his way between commuters until at last he stood at the foot of his building. It was already 8 a.m. when he arrived at his office on the sixty-third floor. His colleagues greeted him with inquiries about the previous evening's date. Despite the fact that Park would never volunteer such information, they had figured it out with just one look at his best suit. Harassing unmarried coworkers over their blind dates was as much a time-honored tradition as the *mat sun* itself.

"So how was it?"

"Fine, I guess."

"What, just fine? We all looked her up online. She's gorgeous."

"Her profile says her hobbies are 'playing the piano' and 'fencing.' What a catch!"

"If you don't want her, I'll take her off your hands."

Park smiled vaguely and sat down at his desk until they went on gossiping on their own. He set down his briefcase, took his meds—the first two pills of the day—and turned on his screen. His first task was always checking the full report of the vitals of the Bio. The oxygen levels were sagging, which needed adjustment—but elsewhere he found that trace gases were unusually and concerningly high. He spent the next hour pulling up more data, and then rushed to talk to his supervisor, the Chief Engineer of the Bureau.

In due silence the Chief Engineer scrutinized the tiny green numbers filling up the black screen. He kept inhaling sharply and audibly through his nose, which appeared necessary to maintain his train of thought when it came to the most serious calculations.

"This amount of carbon monoxide isn't something to be so alarmed about," he said at last.

"But the spike in sulfuric acid?" Park asked hesitantly.

"That's likely from Yellow Day celebrations."

"It's at its highest level in thirty years."

"So what are you thinking, Manager Park?" The Chief Engineer gazed at him steadily.

"I think there is only one plausible explanation. The sand is getting inside the Bio."

"But the air pressure is normal. It's probable that the sulfuric acid number is a fluke. False positive. Based especially on the fact that the number is so high. The Bio contains 20,000 cubic kilometers of atmosphere, carefully calibrated to support life. Even if there is a crack or a fissure somewhere, the amount of sand that can get in wouldn't make any noticeable difference in the air composition for weeks down the road. I thought you were a smart guy," said the Chief Engineer. **99**

"Enough of this. I have other matters to attend to." Then he turned to his screen, effectively ending their conversation.

Park left the office feeling agitated and almost indignant, but the Chief Engineer's argument was hard to refute. Still, he had a hunch that this wasn't just some false positive. When he saw the data, he'd immediately gotten chills down his back. At the end of the day, the Bio was man-made, liable to break down just like anything else.

Over the next week, Park kept a careful watch on the data. After that initial spike, the sulfuric acid levels stayed constant, which appeared to support the Chief Engineer's hypothesis rather than his. Park felt a strange gaping hole in his chest, and became unsettled by the realization that he was incredibly disappointed. It was not because of his ego—he didn't care that someone else was right over him. It also wasn't because he got a twisted, psychotic thrill over the possibility of chaos, destruction, and tragedy. He could only describe it as similar to something being taken from him, a sense of being robbed, though that notion was utterly absurd. Robbed of what, exactly?

Nevertheless, his sense of not-having was so real that he found himself calling Jina for the first time since their date. And yet, the first few exchanges of greeting were so awkward on both sides that he almost wished he could hang up.

Instead, he carried on.

"I was wondering if you wanted to meet," he managed to say.

"For what?"

"I thought that you might like going to a recital." He had looked into music listings and found a recital of a celebrated pianist that weekend. Jina softened as she listened; then they agreed on a time and place to meet, and hung up before either of them could begin to feel awkward again.

The lights slowly darkened and the audience broke into an applause

100 as the pianist was led onto the stage by a young woman. They stopped next to the piano, and he bowed, to more applause; then she pulled out the bench for him and he sat down. The pianist was renowned not just for his virtuosity, but also because he was blind. He'd already been an international concert pianist when he lost his vision, just days before the Bio was finished. When asked in an interview how he adjusted to playing without sight, he had said that he was just doing what he'd always done, seeing the music and the piano keys in his mind. In front of a piano, it was as though he'd never lost his sight.

And as he started playing Beethoven's sonatas, Park was struck by the impression that the pianist really *could* see: not just the piano, but something beyond their reality, the concert hall, their anthracite forest of supertowers and underground malls and apartments like catacombs, every habitable space filled with people or something to support them. No one else objected to this teemingness as far as Park could perceive, but it was all too much and not enough that he sometimes couldn't even stare down his bowl of salad. The pianist wasn't playing for any of that, Park realized—he was playing for that unknowable beyond only he could access. Without meaning to, Park's eyes became hot with tears. For the first time in his life, he felt as though someone had looked into his eyes and said to him, I know what you yearn for.

He closed his eyes and slowed down his breathing so that Jina wouldn't catch him crying. She turned to look at him a few times, but mostly kept her eyes on the pianist, her chin slightly lifted, her posture elegant and proud. Park could tell that she knew all the pieces by the way she seemed to anticipate every change in the theme, and how she smiled slightly before certain passages she liked. That she also loved music gave him hope that they may truly become a couple. He had never had a real relationship before. All of his previous setups by his mother, matchmakers, and online dating companies had fizzled out after a few dates. He had never disliked any of the women, who were all more or less similar: pale, feminine, soft, and a bit anodyne, like cotton candy. The problem was that neither Park nor any of the women could ever muster enough interest to keep going after the first two dates.

Park still didn't know how he felt about Jina, but she seemed different from the others. Underneath her delicate physique, she had something sharp in her. She smoked, and she flirted without giving any indication that she genuinely liked him. She understood music. Park took a sideways glance at her profile and noticed, with pleasure, how she'd made up her eyelashes dramatically with mascara. She was wearing a long silver dress with a low-cut back, which was flattering to her figure. The fact that he took note of her details seemed to be a good sign.

After the recital, they followed the crowd out of the concert hall and onto the plaza. It was another muggy, red-tinged night, but Park wanted to linger there for a moment. The arts center sat on a piney hill in the middle of New Seoul, so it had a view overlooking the entire north side of the city. He led Jina to the edge of the plaza where they leaned out over the balustrade.

"What did you think of the recital?" he asked.

"I thought he was brilliant and sensitive in his own way but also not powerful enough. His style of playing is really much better suited to Chopin," she said. "You must think I'm a snob—it's just that, being a pianist myself, I have different standards than non-musicians do. I also have a more definite idea of how these pieces should be played—having played them myself, and heard so many recordings—that it's hard to overcome certain prejudices."

Park thought she was perfectly justified, and yet he no longer was in the mood to talk about what the music had made him feel. Instead, they both looked out over the city in silence: The supertowers rising nearly to the top of the Bio, and vertical forests and gardens reaching

102   hundreds of stories, all connected by a web of skywalks, monorails, and elevators, and on the ground level the tiny moving figures of electric cars. Everywhere, thousands of neons flashing and pulsating like colorful drum beats. There were so many lights crowded together in this city that there was never any complete darkness unless you covered your face with your hands. Or, unless you were blind. That suddenly struck Park as strange.

"Where do you live?" Jina asked. "Can you see your building?"

Park's building was hidden by the others, but he could point out the general direction of its location.

"Over there, that's my building," Jina pointed to one of the towers. "I'm on the 109th floor. Right about there, where my finger is. What about you?"

"I'm on the fifth floor."

"Goodness, you are practically underground," she said reflexively, sounding disappointed. The best and most expensive apartments were around the hundredth floor, since that was the level of most skywalks and monorails. Jina had never lived below the ninetieth floor in her life, and she wasn't about to start now. Every passing minute she was more convinced that any intrigue she'd initially felt about this man was her acting out in final desperation against ennui. When the matchmaker had presented his profile, her parents had been cautious and unimpressed. Too poor and unconnected, they'd said to her. As an individual he may be your equal, given his educational pedigree, but his family is completely below our family. Still, she'd found something touching about his photo, liked his serious, intelligent eyes under the charcoal black eyebrows; and he'd written down that he was a fan of classical music. But when it came down to it, he was just like every other blind date she's had, just smarter and poorer. She glanced at him out of the corner of her eyes and was freshly annoyed by his thin, slightly concave chest, his spoon-like profile, characteristic of those born before the Bio. As for supposedly being a fan of classical music, he had absolutely nothing to say about the performance, and was just standing there like a statue staring out at the violent lights. So he was one of those boorish men who claimed to know something about music just to flesh out their profiles. Perhaps what had most appealed to her was the chance to frustrate her parents by falling in love with someone who they thought was beneath her. But such capriciousness was costing her her youth. After the night was over, Jina vowed to have an honest conversation with her parents and marry the next eligible match, a younger and richer man who could afford a new apartment in the right district, nowhere near the ground.

As for Park, he was thinking of what one of his colleagues—the junior engineer who offered him one yellow sock—had told a group of them over lunch about his new girlfriend. The guy had said that he and his date were on the monorail when she pointed out her tower, her apartment just a tiny yellow square somewhere in the middle. Every time he passed by it now, he looked at the cluster of windows knowing one of them had her in it, and that made him unbearably happy—and that was how he knew he was in love. Where people live is the most uninteresting, boring fact ever unless it's someone you love, and then it becomes the most imperative thing to know, he claimed sagely. Think about it, he said, do you all remember where I said I live? I've told you all a million times. Or do you actually remember when you run into someone from college and you ask which neighborhood, which building, just to be polite? You know you have no recollection whatsoever after just a day or two. They'd all broken down laughing.

Park had zero interest in knowing where Jina lived.

He looked at her, clad in her thin silvery dress, staring out vacantly into the vast expanse of lights. Nothing could bridge the distance between them, not even standing here together at the edge. He thought about how he would never call her and she'd never call him, and how they would forever disappear from each other's lives.

It was close to midnight by the time he came home. Park washed his face and took his meds—the seventh and eighth pills, the last dosage of the day. The meds had kept him from coughing up bloody phlegm, and made him weak but alive, every day of his life as long as he could remember. Park felt weary, but he still couldn't fall asleep. He turned on the TV and flipped through the channels and stopped when he found the rerun of the Yellow Day public debate program.

"Your argument is based on the assumption that technology doesn't concern morality. But the real moral issue of the Bio is that it eliminates choice," said the literature professor.

"What nonsense—people are free to leave the Bio whenever they like. People travel and go abroad," said the philosopher, smirking. "I've myself just come back from a visiting professorship at the University of ___."

"Then you know well that only the wealthy can travel. How can an average person afford the Bio re-entry fee and the airfare? Effectively, no normal citizen steps outside the Bio in his or her lifetime."

"People always have a choice. It's not always a choice between option A or option B, like at a restaurant. Sometimes you are given just one option, A—but you still have the choice to refuse it," the philosopher said. "In this case, anyone who may wish to do so, for whatever reason, can leave the Bio. There is no Bio exit fee, you might remember, or any law that mandates a citizen stay within a Bio. If you so desire to leave, that is perfectly within your rights, although doing so is clearly against your self-interest. Even a starving person may refuse food. Or one may even refuse to keep breathing, if he so chooses. One has free will and choice at every moment in his life, no matter what circumstances he is in."

"But that is exactly the thing against which I am arguing. A starving person who is offered food doesn't truly have a choice between survival and death. One can only exercise free will when he has a choice between viable options," said the literature professor.

Park got up from the couch. He rushed to get his notepad and pen, and wrote this down:

Morality begins with choice. Without choice there can be no good or evil. There is no freedom here. Without freedom, there can be no meaning.

Without freedom, there can be no love.

When he finished, he read and reread what he wrote. The sense of being wakened to a new consciousness terrified and exhilarated him. On one hand he was filled with tremendous relief at knowing, at last, why it was that he felt so disinterested in his own life. He had never managed to buy into the things that others so naturally believed were important—money, superstitions, marriage, copulation, apartments, and all the other ways in which people proliferated under the Bio like microbes in a petri dish, meaningless and abundant. On the other hand, he still didn't know what he should do. Should he leave? Could he? He knew nothing about life outside the Bio, or any knowledge or skill besides the Bio itself. But that also gave him an enormous advantage: he was one of the few people in the entire city who knew the maintenance exits used periodically by the Department crew—underground passageways that led out a hundred kilometers out to the east, where the mountain range blocks some of the sand. There were still some communities nestled there in the deepest valleys. As recently as several years ago, Park had read some article or another about a handful of farmers who had managed to raise potatoes in the gullies between the mountains and the sea. No one in the Bio still remembered them so they took on the ghostly shapes of hearsay, but without news of any kind Park had

106 to assume that they still lived.

Whether he could actually follow through with this was another matter. Perhaps in the morning his resolution would fail, his lungs would collapse, and he would resign himself to obeying the Bio's rules without struggle. There was a chance that some hideous punishment was already being prepared for his insubordination. But somewhere he could hear and was soothed by the arpeggio notes of a deaf composer. So there was just one thing he could do in the here and the now. With a smile, he closed his eyes and waited to be swept away by the wind. ❧

Juhea Kim's writing has been published in Granta, Times Literary Supplement, Joyland, *and other publications. Her first novel,* Beasts of a Little Land, *will be published in the fall by Ecco.*

THINKING ABOUT PLACE WHEN THINKING ABOUT TECH: A CONVERSATION WITH XIAOWEI WANG

JOHN MCMURTRIE

Much of what we in the West are told about China and its phenomenal economic growth centers on the so-called first-tier cities—the booming metropolises of Beijing, Guangzhou, and Shanghai and their gleaming, seemingly come-out-of-nowhere skylines.

But what about the countryside? China is a historically agrarian society, and forty percent of its population still lives in rural areas. That's equivalent to eight percent of the world's population—and twice the population of the United States.

Xiaowei Wang decided to find out more about this often-overlooked segment of the world's second-largest economy. Wang grew up in the Boston area, and even though they have relatives who live in the Chinese countryside, they admit to not having known much about life outside of the country's big cities. So Wang, a former coder, set out to challenge themselves in their first book, *Blockchain Chicken Farm: And Other Stories of Tech in China's Countryside*. Wang completed it while working on their PhD in geography at UC Berkeley.

108   *Blockchain Chicken Farm* is a short book—only 248 pages long—but it provides an impressive and sweeping overview of an increasingly stratified nation and its fraught relationship with technological change. It's also a personal account, as well as a probing, philosophical inquiry into China's future. The blockchain of the book's title refers to the complex record-keeping system whose most famous use is Bitcoin. But this is far from a sterile book about facts and figures. People are at the heart of this story.

"Why are you here?" the author writes in the book's introduction. "I am here because looking at technology in rural China, in places that produce the technology we use, places that show how globally entangled we are with one another, allows me to confront the scarier question that technology poses: What does it mean to live, to be human right now?"

The following conversation took place over Zoom in January.

JOHN MCMURTRIE: I want to start with the title of your book: *Blockchain Chicken Farm*. It gets your attention and it also illustrates so much about the dynamic between technology and tradition-al, rural life in China. So let's talk about these forty-dollar chickens. What are they, and how did you first hear about them?

XIAOWEI WANG: I actually found out about them through my aunt, who lives in Guangzhou. She's one of these upper-class urbanites who spends a lot of time shopping on-line. There's such a robust grocery delivery system in Chinese cities beyond what we have here. You can buy one small thing, and it'll be at your door within an hour or two. There's also this high price on food safety because there's been a lot of contamination and food safety scandals in the past.

So it's a chicken that's available on JD.com and it has like a chicken Fitbit with a QR code that you can scan. You can see how many steps the chicken has walked. It's like this surveilled chicken. So I de-cided that I would go to the village that was raising these blockchain chickens, and it became clear that blockchain chicken was just this marketing scheme. It was made by this Shanghai technology company.

JM: To some people, this idea of blockchain chicken might seem attractive—you can track your chicken and know everything about it. It had me thinking of a *Portlandia* episode in which an earnest and doubting couple at a restaurant wants to know everything about the chicken they're going to eat, and whether it's organic. And the server assures them that it is organic, and she shows them a picture of the chicken, saying, "His name was Colin."

But as "innovative" as the blockchain chicken system might seem, it's actually based on the assumption that the government can't be trusted. That's where private industry—a big e-commerce giant like Alibaba—comes in. People start placing their faith in companies instead. What problems does that pose?

XW: This is the eternal problem, which is that the issues of food security in China are caused by a privatized market industry of agriculture, meaning that these big agribusiness companies are trying to make the most profit possible. They really squeeze these small farmers that are producing for them. And the small farmers are like, Well, I guess we kind of need to cheat. We have a lot of pressure. And then conveniently, a lot of these large corporations also have this solution of, you know, buy your forty-dollar chicken on JD.com. Alibaba, they're this big tech company in China, but they have their own supermarket now. And it really banks on food safety, food security—"we guarantee everything is fresh, you can see the employees working to package things every day." It's a level of surveillance sold as comfort.

JM: What made you decide to focus your story on China's countryside?

XW: I was visiting Shenzhen, this electronics hub, this huge city. And I was talking to someone

110 who runs the Open Innovation Lab there, David Li. And he said you could just continue to go to the cities, but that's the boring story. No one's going into the countryside, where there's this long history of tech industrialization and modernization efforts, and also these inventive ways that a lot of Chinese farmers are starting to incorporate tech. Things kind of flowed from there, over multiple trips. Some villages I visited quite a few times throughout the course of a few years.

JM: How much did you know about the countryside before you started visiting it?

XW: My mom's side of the family—they're, I guess, the English term is country bumpkins [laughs]. Visiting my mom's family in the countryside was similar to a lot of what people express—you're just like, Okay, never going to visit the countryside again! [laughs]. It's just starkly different.

JM: But your perspective must have changed dramatically after researching the book, which defi-

nitely has an appreciation for so many of these people who live there.

XW: Yes, and I think for a lot of urban folks now, the attitude is, Oh, we have to bring these country folks into the present or the future. And that's a really problematic way of thinking about it.

JM: Then there's "re-peasantization." Is that the term?

XW: Yes. I think it's happening in the U.S. a little bit, too. Some people call it rural gentrification. It's a generation of young folks who say maybe it is better if we just go back and raise our own chickens and food. It's an interesting dynamic. It's also setting up tensions. I visited one village where they have the equivalent of an Airbnb now. And they want tourists. And the older generation thinks, This is nice, but it's kind of not really helping us. We feel like a zoo now.

JM: One of the many things I learned from your book is that China, the world's biggest pork producer, has a pork reserve, just as the U.S. has wheat reserves, in case of famine. The industrial pig farm you write about is one of the more disturbing stories you include. Tell us about it.

XW: I wanted to visit an industrial hog farm. But I was told by multiple people at that time that it's

tecting if a pig is sick or not. The high biosecurity is because if one pig gets sick, they're in such close quarters that the illness will just tear through the entire farm.

JM: I had never heard of pig facial recognition before reading your book.

> *"I go on to Amazon and see all these knockoffs— even for things like tents, sleeping bags—with these English-sounding names. And I always get the sense that they come from one of these Taobao villages or 'e-commerce villages."*

impossible. There was, you know, ASF—African Swine Fever—going around; it was basically a huge biosecurity crisis. Even under normal circumstances, you would have to quarantine before going into the hog farm. So I started to look into it: why is there such a high level of biosecurity? It turns out that the pigs are raised under these conditions where it really is a factory. Alibaba is trying to scale up this pork production even more by using sensors, cameras, all these automated ways of de-

XW: Exactly. It's to track the different pigs, make sure they're not sick, monitor them for health. Because one human can't look at a thousand pigs and always have a sense of whether they're healthy or not.

JM: You also traveled to northern China, to a place called Dinglou. It's the country's first Taobao Village. What's the place like?

XW: You know, it's weird going on Amazon these days. They've made it very easy for foreign sellers outside of the U.S. to sell di-

112 rectly on their site. I don't know if others see this, but after going to Dinglou, I can't unsee it. So I go on to Amazon and see all these knockoffs—even for things like tents, sleeping bags—with these English-sounding names. And I always get the sense that they come from one of these Taobao villages or "e-commerce villages."

At this point, there are a couple thousand of them, if not more. Alibaba has this platform called Taobao, which is sort of like eBay or Amazon. It's all products that are new. And in these villages, they're just manufacturing things and selling them on Taobao. It's taken off in recent years with farmers who are trying to find new sources of income, young folks who are going back to their ancestral villages and rural areas to find new things to do that aren't farming. It's getting really expensive to manufacture in Chinese cities. But it's super cheap in the countryside. It's really small, like making things in your garage and then putting them on Amazon to sell. But some of these villages, they become whole ecosystems.

In Dinglou, they were making Halloween costumes, but knockoff Halloween costumes. So it'd be like Snow White, but not quite Snow White. And, you know, you have your neighbor who is running an embroidery business, and this other person who's doing screen printing. This has become common throughout China in many places. People rely on their families for these businesses. I would go into cellars where grandmothers who are ninety years old are putting labels on packages.

JM: Could you see something similar happening in the U.S., that this country might have Amazon villages or, if not Amazon, some other company down the road?

XW: Throughout the course of researching this book I talked to this person from the Center on Rural Innovation in the U.S. And he was saying rural economic development here is, "Let's build a slaughterhouse or a prison." And that's it. There are no other imaginative possibilities that give people anything.

I think in rural China, especially the type of villages that I visited, it's a very different relationship to economic development. In China, rural revitalization is like an official national government policy. So even though we think of China as authoritarian, it leaves a lot up to the different provinces as well.

I also feel like rural America has its own particular flavor of entitlement—even with the farm crisis where people stopped farming and lost land and had to take up these random jobs. It's this combination of white supremacy and entitlement that crafts and shapes what you feel like you're entitled to.

JM: You write about the pearl industry, too. I don't think I'll ever be able to look at pearls in quite the same way.

XW: I stumbled across this phenomenon of pearl parties on Facebook Live, where basically a lot of white women in Trump-voting states open up these oysters on Facebook livestream and then sell them for ten dollars each as cheap jewelry. I started doing some research into this and found out where these oysters came from. There's this whole kind of gory story—they actually harvest these pearls from a larger oyster and then put them into these smaller oysters and then ship off the smaller oysters in formaldehyde to the U.S. to fuel this pearl party online phenomenon. I visited one of the oyster farms, and they were very excited by my visit. They opened up a couple oysters for me when I was there. I got to open one. They'd neglected to tell me that they feed it chicken and pig feces. So that was a surprise.

JM: One solution to food safety and the equitable treatment of workers is an organic rice cooperative in southern China, in Guangdong village. The system seems ingenious, and it benefits everyone. Could such a model be replicated with other farms, possibly avoiding the need for larger industrial places?

XW: It is this beautiful system. With the rice paddy system that

114

they have, you each get a paddy. And because it's a natural form of irrigation, the water flows from the top to the bottom of the terrace. As a result, you would shoot yourself in the foot if you dam off and collect all the water at the top—your paddy at the bottom wouldn't get any water. So the distribution of paddies is done on a lottery system. It's a communal system. And they rotate every five years to make sure you're tied into the system with each other.

In terms of if it's replicable, I think it is, but it always takes that sustained community effort. And for this particular community, they've been open to outsiders coming in and staying with them for a few years, helping be part of this process. They've also been open to selling their rice online and making rice wine. They're still going, even through the pandemic. It's very heartening.

JM: When you were a child in Boston, you helped your aunt sell Chinese wares at a street stall. One day, you overheard an American speak contemptuously about anything made in China—that it was cheap. His words stayed with you. Do you think Americans' attitudes about Chinese goods have changed?

XW: No, I think it's gotten even worse. I was out near the Delta [near Sacramento], and I saw a truck that had this sticker that said "Boycott Made in China." And honestly, it was my first time seeing one of those, and I go to places around NorCal a lot.

JM: Donald Trump made China the boogeyman of his candidacy, then his presidency—first by accusing China of being an unfair trading partner and then by deflecting attention about the raging coronavirus pandemic in this country by lashing out at China and what he called the "China virus." Do you have a sense of how people in China will view Joe Biden?

XW: I think folks in China are relieved, because the anxiety of military tensions was also real. Already just talking to friends who are in the China policy sphere,

I think there's much more of a smarter China strategy with the Biden administration, which is forming these coalitions between here and Europe to pressure China on its human rights abuses. And actually examining the fine detail of how these Chinese companies are going to be regulated instead of just ineffectually banning them through an executive order. I think there's some optimism both here that Trump put in power, I hope they'll kind of trickle out and leave, and we'll get a new generation of policymakers. Just changing the rhetoric. But I also think there's a level of weird misunderstanding. To put it more bluntly, a lot of it is just racism, right? People saying things like, "Oh, yeah, it's the China virus or the kung flu."

JM: It's impressive how you've been able to pursue so many varied

> *"I think culturally we'll be left with the effects of the Trump administration for a long time. I don't know if U.S.-China relations will ever recover from that."*

and also in China about the new administration. At the same time, I think culturally we'll be left with the effects of the Trump administration for a long time. I don't know if U.S.-China relations will ever recover from that.

JM: What are some of the things that could be done to help better those relations?

XW: A lot of the policymakers who are at the State Department interests. You're a former software engineer, you're an artist and writer, a landscape architect, you're getting your PhD. And you're the creative director of *Logic*, a magazine about technology that's based in San Francisco. How do you navigate these passions?

XW: It doesn't feel like different aspects of my brain. I feel like I just want to learn and know more, constantly.

116 **JM:** What's the focus of your PhD?

XW: Geography. I went in doing more dry, quantitative, spatial simulation modeling stuff, but my adviser moved back to New Zealand because he said America is a capitalist hellhole.

JM: What did you tell your adviser at that point?

XW: I was like, "Oh, you're probably right." [laughs] But he also had two kids who needed to go to college for free in New Zealand. So I took a detour, and without having an adviser around, ended up just reading a lot of post-colonial theory and stuff about global development. In tech, we talk about information and tech as if the digital were this other sphere, and if users just modeled the perfect behavior of an online network then we would be better, rational, more informed citizens. It's always this abstract. Geography says, no, you have to think about place. You have to think about political economy. You have to think about these material relations. I think that grounded view is really important, especially in tech.

JM: And how did you become involved in community empowerment work?

XW: After undergrad, after living in New York for a while, things weren't really working out with the jobs in the U.S., so I moved to China. I started working on more urban gardening and ecology work in the community and thinking about community gardens there, land reform, agriculture. I started doing these public art and community-based workshops, where I was getting people to measure air quality using these sensors. It continues to be fulfilling. I love talking to people

"Kite flying is such a core of Chinese urban life, so it was a way to be playful but also gather this interesting community."

and learning things from others.

JM: Tell us more about the sensors.

XW: That was my first big community empowerment public art project. It was these air quality sensors that people could attach to kites. Kite flying is such a core of Chinese urban life, so it was a way to be playful but also gather this interesting community—old Beijing residents, younger university students, people who you think would normally, quote unquote, not care about the environment.

JM: With the pandemic, I'm guessing you haven't traveled much lately. When do you hope to return to China?

XW: Apparently, some people are going there. But I don't know. I just don't feel like I can responsibly make that decision to go. But I miss it terribly. &<

John McMurtrie is the former books editor of the San Francisco Chronicle. *His writing has appeared in* The New York Times, The Los Angeles Times, *and Literary Hub.*

THE POET

SHERYL LUNA

for Martin Balgach

He is an astronomer
measuring the distance
between light and loneliness,
time and silence, the sound of his voice
and the dreams of millions.
There are constellations in his eyes,
and orphaned poems fill his days.
He holds his face in his palms every night.
Universes wander inside him. He feels
himself a black hole, space, the extraterrestrial
other. The real mystery is love and he
deems the indifferent galaxies expanding
forever into nothingness, a kind of perfect
stillness. He calculates wishes
and lost dreams, draws conclusions
and arguments based on hunger and the empty
stomach of humanity. The moon is an idea
and light shimmers on the rough water
of himself, running into a sea gray
with the polluted madness of want.
He believes in firecrackers, the supernova
of desire's fight against time, but he knows
it's all a lie. There is the rumor
of salvation. He wants to hold on

to the last warmth of the sun,

to believe his small yelp matters,

that the Milky Way mourns his passing,

burns stardust while his hands are lit

with a million years of truth.

. . . .

Sheryl Luna is the author of the poetry collections Pity the Drowned Horses *(University of Notre Dame Press),* Seven *(3: A Taos Press), and* Magnificent Hours, *forthcoming from University of Notre Dame Press in 2022.*

ARTIST'S NOTES

DAVE MCCLINTON

I combine my love of photography, art, and graphic design to create works that speak to the viewer by communicating something specific and clear, while also harboring subtexts that reward repeated viewing or discussion. My work as a graphic designer has been to communicate quickly and efficiently through logo and branding work—and I believe that same economy of message can be applied to art.

I use textures, archival images, family photos, found imagery, and self-portraiture to create unique faces that tell the story of the Black American experience. Within the African American culture, we are rediscovering our history—a history that has not been fully illustrated. My role as a visual communicator is to review historical information and inform the community by bringing these concepts to life, helping to visually define our identity. Distributing these stories about the strengths and trials of the African American community is a big part of my motivation.

I want to illustrate the journey of a Black person's inner life. From innocent to informed. From recklessly defiant to determined. How the weight of American history can either crush you or harden you. And how either result has to be hidden from view just to get through the day.

I want the community to seize this moment in history to create and discuss work that tells a story and compels them to seek out empathy and activism for the sake of others. My hope is the work I'm creating can help do that. I want to spark conversations that have, historically, been hard to start.

DAVE MCCLINTON

Couldn't Help Myself, 2018, digital collage
courtesy: the artist

DAVE MCCLINTON

Bro Haha, 2018, digital collage
courtesy: the artist

DAVE MCCLINTON

Perp Petual, 2016, digital collage
courtesy: the artist

DAVE MCCLINTON

Hard Livin' I, 2016, digital collage
courtesy: the artist

DAVE MCCLINTON

Harper in Service, 2017, digital collage
courtesy: the artist

DAVE MCCLINTON

Ola, 2017, digital collage
courtesy: the artist

Overthrow, 2019, digital collage
courtesy: the artist

DAVE MCCLINTON

Plaid Yourself, 2019, digital collage
courtesy: the artist

MR. PINK

KATE REED PETTY

To keep the women straight, Owen based them on characters from *Reservoir Dogs*. Madeleine Pink was selfish. Hillary Brown was a know-it-all nerd. Jasmine Blonde was charming but super mean. Alexis White was competent, cool. And Jen Orange was fucking Beretta.

He image searched for profile pics with subtle mnemonics: Alexis was a bouquet of white flowers, Madeleine the paint swatch for Pantone 205. He put all five women in L.A., though Jen spent half the year in New York. He had them each follow 700 of the people who followed him.

Then Owen spent the rest of Saturday morning writing hundreds of posts, so that their accounts would look human, and sympathetic, and real.

✻　✻　✻

He'd made his first fake account Friday night. "TravisBickle4587." Just a cool, generic guy, a smart and cynical nobody who posted about movies, and what he ate for lunch, and why Owen Kane was innocent.

Owen chose "Travis Bickle" because it was something a typical movie guy would choose. He didn't want the account to stand out.

But he also liked what the character stood for. Travis Bickle was a flawed dude, definitely, but this was a flawed world. Travis Bickle understood

130 about ends and means and righteousness and being justified.

For Travis's profile pic, Owen chose the famous still from the end of *Taxi Driver*, DeNiro covered in blood with a finger-gun pointed at his own head. The image was one of Owen's favorites.

Travis wrote *hello world.*

Owen leaned back and tried to think of something else. He was fresh off a short, circular phone call with his manager that had not gone well. His manager was supposed to be helping him but wasn't—maybe couldn't—but whatever, Owen just needed some sympathy.

Travis wrote *SWINGERS is the best movie ever made, come @ me bro.*

Travis wrote *Okay here's my #minutemoviepitch: SOME LIKE IT HOT meets DIE HARD, two hostages in drag must stop a bank heist.*

Then Owen realized that was a pretty good idea. Travis deleted the post so no one would steal it.

Owen opened a new browser to scroll through his own feed for inspiration. But everyone who was smart and cared about movies was posting about Owen and the now-five women he'd offended. Owen logged out.

Allegedly offended.

Owen stared at the blinking cursor on Travis's account. He suddenly felt stupid for thinking that Travis could help him. What was Travis doing hanging out on social media on a Friday night? Travis was a creep and a perv.

What Owen needed was some women standing up for him.

❁   ❁   ❁

MR. PINK

He used burner email accounts to register them. He gave them all the same password—URAG00dManOwenKane!—which his computer told him was very strong.

He named them after a clique of girls who'd lived in his freshman hall. Madeleine Hillary Jasmine Alexis and Jen.

He hadn't seen those girls since sophomore year. But he still thought about them, sometimes. They were mean and funny and everyone always hung out in their rooms. Even now, fifteen years out of college, when he thought about power he thought about them.

They overflowed between two dorm rooms, five girls tessellated on top of each other. Long limbs under towels running to and from the showers. Piles of clothes on every bed, like too many pillows in a luxury hotel.

He wanted them to notice him, that's all. Like they noticed the acoustic guitar guy. Or the soccer guy. Or the gay guy. Or the other acoustic guitar guy. But when Owen made a joke they ignored him. When he repeated it louder, they said *yeah, we heard you the first time.*

Recently, at a mall, Owen passed a store overflowing with body lotion, and the smell of fake flowers wafting out the door sent him spiraling through arousal and nausea, hating himself. That old familiar feeling.

So this is despair, he used to tell himself, on any given weeknight when he emerged from that dorm room, the sound of everyone's laughter closing the door behind him.

Except that one time. He'd brought pot brownies. And after they were all high he started talking about porn, how they should put some porn on. Both of the acoustic guitar guys agreed. They joked about it until the girls agreed, too.

132 Owen remembered that moment so clearly: sitting over one of the girl's computers, his fingers curled over the search bar like a gargoyle, hesitating.

Not because he didn't know the video he wanted. He was hesitating because he wasn't sure what to type. He didn't want his search terms to give it away. He wanted them unprepared. He wanted them nauseated and aroused.

What's taking so long, Owen? one of the girls said. Another said, *No girl's ever said* THAT *to Owen before,* and everyone laughed.

Owen just chuckled pleasantly. He'd have his revenge.

Forty-five seconds into the video they kicked him out of the room. The walls of the hallway throbbed under his hands as he made his way back to his single. He had not realized that he was so very high.

He lay on his narrow bed and dreamed about his future life, his real life, when he would tell the story of the time he tricked the mean girls into watching disgusting porn.

✳   ✳   ✳

Now here he was again, his fingers again hovering over the keyboard, again unsure of the words he wanted to use.

The problem was he couldn't remember what those five girls from college were like. They were gauzy, always laughing, out of reach. The first posts he wrote sounded flat and bitter. He deleted them.

He opened another window and started scrolling. *The Oscars Kanye the Ghostbusters with girls in it. The betrayal! A joke about feeling insecure in Thai restaurants Mercury in retrograde a rant about plane travel*

The opening scene of Reservoir Dogs. Owen clicked and Quentin Tarantino's voice reached out to him, talking about Madonna.

The scene dawned on him, comfortable as a third beer with an old friend. A group of thieves, in a diner, jostling with each other. Who was moral, who was a man. *"Like a Virgin" is about big dicks.*

This was a movie about power, but this was a fair fight. This was a movie about power, and how you could earn it by being smart.

Madeleine Pink. Hillary Brown. Jasmine Blonde. Alexis White. And Jen Orange was fucking Beretta.

❊   ❊   ❊

After that it was easy.

Madeleine and Alexis wrote competing reviews of a popular streaming TV series. Madeleine said it was overproduced and pulpy, Alexis said that was the point.

Jasmine made jokes about writer's block. Hillary complained about politics. Jen posted about a trip to a farmers' market where she spent too much money on subpar baked goods. *They were baked bads,* she posted.

Owen giggled about that for the rest of the day. "Baked bads," he said to himself, shaking his head, as his lunch steadily rotated in the microwave.

Alexis shared a post by a film critic who called himself the Hulk. Jen shared a post about a news satire show. Madeleine shared a post by a cynical comedian. Jasmine shared a bunch of posts by right-wingers and added *just jacking off!* to all of them. Hillary shared a post by Alexis.

By Saturday night they'd each gained at least a hundred followers. Jasmine and Jen had the most, with 340 and 282, respectively.

134   All five of the women shared posts from Owen Kane, adding little LOLs or just the word "this" with an emoji of a pointed finger.

It made Owen want to check his own account. Because he'd logged out Friday night, he had to click the little box to prove that *I am not a robot.* Then he had to wait for a text message with a six-digit code. Then he was in.

But he'd forgotten that he was now getting dozens of notifications every hour. His account unspooled down his screen and into a bottomless pit, a swarm tangling up and around itself, suggesting Owen Kane receive medieval punishments.

For what crime? Owen was an asshole. He knew that. But everyone was an asshole. This wasn't fair at all.

He logged out. He did fifteen pushups. He did a breathing exercise.

He sent his manager an email, saying that he was just going to keep his head down and finish the screenplay. *I'm working all weekend,* he said. Then he felt much better. He logged back into the women's accounts.

❋   ❋   ❋

By Sunday afternoon each of his women had really found her voice. Hillary was going by Hills. Alexis was writing clever haiku. Jasmine never capitalized anything, UNLESS SHE CAPITALIZED EVERYTHING. Madeleine used a lot of emoji.

Jen was his favorite. She was really funny and smart. She had gone through and liked all of Owen's #minutemoviepitches from the past year.

Owen was proud of himself. He'd been struggling over the same screenplay—*The Apartment* reimagined as a high school rom-com— since moving to New York last year. He was forty pages into the script and had been stuck there for months.

Madeleine Hillary Jasmine Alexis and Jen made him feel like he was on vacation with new friends. Friends that everyone liked. He watched their follower counts climb.

In the afternoon he made himself take a break. He walked to the coffee shop to treat himself to a mocha.

"Baked bads," he said, waiting in line, chuckling to himself over the pastries lined up in the glass case. He realized there was another joke in there. He tried to think of a pun about cooking meth. *Cookie meth?* Something like that.

A warm breeze blew in through the windows of the coffee shop and he was suffused with the feeling that things were going to be okay. He smiled at the girl who always took his order. "Large mocha for here," he said, leaning slightly toward her.

He came here most days. He usually made her laugh. He planned to ask her out one day. She had hair dyed electric blue and a neck tattoo. *She was fucking Beretta!* He realized it as he waited for her to acknowledge him. Maybe today he would ask her out.

But she wasn't looking at him. Owen stared at her for a long awkward minute before he realized that she was not going to look at him. "You can take your card out," she said to the floor. She rotated the face of the digital pad toward Owen, and turned her own face beyond him.

"What can I get you?" she said, her warmth a sudden spotlight pointed at the next person in line.

Owen hit the screen where it said *custom tip*. He left her twenty dollars. Then instead of signing in the blank space on the digital pad, he wrote

136   *fuck you bitch.*

He left his mocha on the counter and walked out. He was eager to get home anyway. He had things to do. He was in the best part of the writing process. The characters were doing unexpected things. He wanted to see what they would say next.

Alexis wrote: *The end of this film / oh my god oh my / god this sucks,* about *Passengers,* which Owen liked, actually.

Jasmine wrote *i really respect that the q-tip marketing slogan is* VARIETY OF USES. *i've been in such a q-tip rut. ear cleaning only.* I CAN'T BELIEVE I'M WASTING MY Q-TIPS' POTENTIAL. Which was just weird, although it got 67 likes.

Madeleine wrote *I want to remake* THEY LIVE *but set in modern-day tech-drowned San Francisco.* Owen disagreed. He strongly disagreed.

Owen disagreed with Madeleine so vehemently he logged into his own account to respond. He ignored the angry red notification bell at the top, and just started writing. *Remake* THEY LIVE*?! Sacrilege!! Next you'll be telling me you want to remake it with an all female cast.*

Then he remembered that he wasn't supposed to be on social media for a while, and deleted it.

Hills dug up Travis Bickle's post about *Swingers* and reposted it with a comment, *Imagine being a straight white man #nostalgia #barf.* Madeleine agreed, posting the emoji for rolling your eyes.

Then Alexis agreed, too, posting something about the Bechdel test.

Jen responded *No way, Swingers holds up #vegasbaby.* Jen really was his favorite, God love her.

But still. Owen sat for a minute, imagining what it would like to be Travis, reading that post, reading everything the women had said about him. He imagined Travis wouldn't care. Travis would write *fuck you bitch* and keep going. Travis was a creep and a perv.

Owen opened a new browser window and deleted Travis's account. He didn't need Travis. He liked the women so much.

✶   ✶   ✶

There were programs he could have used to manage all of the women's accounts simultaneously; he could have been scheduling things to post throughout the day, so that he didn't have to be so involved.

Instead he kept five different browser programs open, each in privacy mode, and routed through the VPN he'd set up while researching a pitch for a spy film last year. He was paranoid about getting caught.

Plus it felt pretty cool to have five browsers open like that. Monday morning when he sat down at his desk with a cup of coffee he felt like the stoic, competent Captain in a space epic, like he was driving the rebel ship in *The Matrix*.

He felt important, and in control, and he knew that today was the day the women were going to break their silence about Owen Kane.

Jen went first. *I've been agonizing all weekend over whether to say this. Owen is an old friend, and I'm heartbroken over the accusations against him. He deserves a fair hearing, innocent until proven guilty.*

Owen leaned back and looked at that for a long time. He blinked tears. "Thanks, Jenny," he said.

Alexis liked the post, and then Hills, and then two other strangers, too. Owen was encouraged.

MR. PINK

138 A little later Hills responded, *I still think he's sexy. In that Christian-Slater-in-Heathers serious bad-boy kind of way.*

Then Hills responded to her own post, *Not to belittle a serious matter. I'm just saying, with Owen, you know what you're getting into, the dark edge is part of the fun.*

Then Alexis said *I agree, I've never seen Owen do anything disrespectful, he's just joking around sometimes. I'm not sure about all of this.*

The tide of posts about Owen started swelling. *Did you even read the accusations* and *I read his first script, it's obvious he hates women* and all kinds of other unfair things. But also level-headed responses.

It's not like he's Harvey Weinstein, people said.

Madeleine and Alexis joined in, pointed out the danger of *things going too far,* said *both sides need to be heard.*

I don't know Owen that well, but he has always been supportive of my work and totally gentlemanly, Jasmine finally chimed in.

But nobody paid her much attention, because there were hundreds of other posts, spinning away. Momentum was gaining. Complexity was increasing. What was once a chorus was now an argument.

He leaned back at the desk of his starship, navigating this strange world, and felt a warm, buzzing feeling of relief in his chest. Maybe he would make it back alive.

✳ ✳ ✳

Tuesday morning, *The Apartment* as a high-school rom-com stared back at Owen from the big white space on page 41, empty and bitter. He missed Madeleine and Hills and Jasmine and Alexis and Jen.

MR. PINK

He decided to write one post from each of the women. Just as a way to get the creative juices flowing. Then he would get back to the screenplay. He would finish the screenplay today, he just needed to get the juices flowing first.

He opened his five browser windows and stretched out his fingers over the keyboard and typed URAG00dManOwenKane! in the box under Jen's name.

His computer flashed back at him in red text, as if irritated. *The username and password you entered do not match our records. Please double-check and try again.*

Owen tried again. *The username and password you entered do not match our records. Please double-check and try again.*

He switched to another browser and tried Hills, and then Madeleine. It was the same. And the same for Alexis and Jasmine.

Forgot Password? he clicked, and the browser promised it was sending him an email.

But then he couldn't get into his burner email accounts. *Wrong password. Try again or click Forgot Password to reset it.*

He logged into his own email. That password worked. He had a response from his manager, from the note he'd sent Saturday night: *Great, Owen, can't wait to read the new script!* and the thumbs-up emoji. Owen didn't really think that was helpful.

Owen switched over to his own social account. He ignored the alarm bell icon—now 3,746 notifications red—because he was staring at the post at the top of his feed.

At one o'clock in the morning the night before, Jen had posted *Can't sleep, quick can you guys send me as many cute photos of sleeping kittens as possible?* Owen was definitely asleep at one o'clock.

And then like thirty people had sent Jen pictures of kittens. Jen had spent the next hour responding to all of them with variations of *awww adorable* and *thank you this helps!*

As Owen stared, a new post appeared. Jasmine wrote *some personal news: i've decided to become a brand, from now on please call me JASMINE! the exclamation point is mandatory.*

Owen stood up from his desk, knocking his chair over. He turned and went into the bathroom and splashed water on his face. He did a breathing exercise. He got into the shower and let the water run as hot as he could stand it.

He wiped a circle into the steam on the mirror and stood looking at himself. He would use this one day, he reminded himself. He would use all of this in a script. Nothing bad could really happen to a writer because a real writer could make anything into art.

He did fifteen pushups and then went back out and sat down at his computer and tried, again, to log into the women's accounts, but he didn't know the words to use.

Wrong password, the internet said. *Try again?*

✿   ✿   ✿

Hours later he was still staring at his computer screen, the setting sun casting long shadows from the beer cans piled up around his desk.

The women were all talking without him.

Alexis posted about a sold-out concert she wanted to go to, *does anyone have tickets?* Owen had never heard of the band.

Hills described a new perfume she kept smelling on strangers, *like overripe peaches in a room where someone smoked a joint half an hour ago, can anyone tell me what it is?* Owen did not like when women wore perfume.

Madeleine posted *There are SO MANY badass Latinx folks doing comedy in LA and generally being awesome, I feel like we need to rally, can we start an annual get-together to celebrate each other's awesomeness?* Owen had thought all of the women were white.

Jasmine found a vintage commercial for cigarettes, *is it just me or does this look like an ad for the lesbian lifestyle?* Jen responded *Once you got the bug, EVERYTHING is an ad for the lesbian lifestyle.* Which, like, what did that even mean?

Jen posted *I have to go to the DMV today, what can I expect?* Hills replied. *It's like the red bathroom in THE SHINING* with a screenshot meme captioned *You've always been the Caretaker.* Which normally would have made Owen laugh.

They were hanging out, having a great time. They were fine with him sitting there, listening. They posted all around him, friendly teasing phrases that didn't mean anything. He kept thinking of things he wanted to say but he was afraid to speak up.

He kept getting up and standing in the middle of the kitchen as if he was going to make himself something to eat but he didn't want to eat anything.

He did fifteen push-ups. He did a breathing exercise. He thought of punching a hole in the wall, but he was too afraid to try, because what if he couldn't do it? He had written a lot of characters punching holes

142   in walls but had never actually done it himself.

He walked back toward his computer and he was hit by a wave of shame so powerful he couldn't breathe. He held on to the back of his chair and gasped. Madeleine Jasmine Hills Alexis and Jen knew him, his women *knew him.* They weren't like the others, the crowd online that had projected their own values and politics onto a few skimpy hysterical accusations from old mistakes, the unfair thrashing mob screaming for Owen's head. These women were his friends and lovers. He had laughed with them, confided in them, had trusted them to carry him through this hard time in his life. He thought he could trust them. But he didn't know them. He didn't know whether they understood him, what they thought about him. He didn't know them at all.

✻ ✻ ✻

Madeleine was the first to turn on him.

I've been thinking a lot about the accusations against Owen Kane, and I feel really terrible about the way I reacted to them.

Owen stood up at his desk as he read it.

I tried to defend Owen because he's a friend and I thought I owed him that, but I've come to see that his behavior is unforgivable.

Hills wrote *Me, too. I've been talking to a lot of the women who had bad experiences with Owen Kane. I believe them. I'm sorry I was myopic before.*

Alexis liked it and added *I've changed my mind, too.*

Jasmine liked it and added *you think you know someone, turns out he's a MOTHERFUCKER like ALL THE REST.*

He watched Jen's account, holding his breath. For a while she was quiet.

MR. PINK

Then: *Hey guys,* she wrote. *This is really hard.*

Then she reposted the accusations, one after the other. He knew these things. He hadn't looked at them since last week. But he knew them by heart. One was from a crazy person he had made the mistake of dating for three months. One was a crazy person he had made the mistake of hooking up with once. One was a very level-headed, cold person who hated him. One was a very insecure person who was apparently comfortable lying and who wanted to fit in. One was a very lovely person who must have felt some kind of loyalty to the others. All of the things they said were technically true, if you looked at just the bare facts. You couldn't argue with the facts. But it was the very story that was untrue, it was the way the women interpreted the facts. It was the way they reacted that were lies.

Jen had reposted them all. All of the accusations, in full. And after each one she had added her own accusation. *Same threat to me,* she said. *Same violent grab.*

That was just messing around!! Owen typed, and then deleted, and then typed and deleted again, a hundred times.

I didn't do anything wrong. Deleted.

These are the kinds of things that just happen. Deleted.

It wasn't fair to call him out, and only him, *when men do these kinds of things all the fucking time.* Deleted.

What about the girls who made fun of my sexual stamina in college? What about the producer who said she could tell from Owen's writing that Owen was an incompetent lover? Deleted. Deleted.

Delete your account, said Madeleine and Hillary and Jasmine and Alexis.

144   And Jen was fucking Beretta. *You need to apologize, Owen,* she said.

Fuck you bitch, he wrote back.

✻   ✻   ✻

He deleted the post, too late.

This is what I'm talking about, Jen wrote, with a screen captured image of Owen's last post. He watched as dozens of people reposted it. And then hundreds. The red bell at the top of his screen screamed in alarm.

He closed his computer like punching a hole in the wall. Then he went out and sat in his car and gripped the steering wheel until his knuckles turned white and he knew he needed to apologize. He got out of the car and walked back up to his apartment and went straight to the computer, not even turning on the lights. He stared at the empty white box with his fingers hunched over the keyboard. He didn't know the words you were supposed to say. *I'm sorry,* he wrote, but it sounded so dumb. He deleted it.

He opened a new search box, and typed *the ending of Reservoir Dogs.* He found a video clip of the last five minutes of the movie, starting with the Mexican standoff.

He watched it five times. Every time, it made him sob. Every time, when he got to the very end—Mr. Orange gasping in a puddle of blood, confessing his betrayal to his closest friend—Owen had to wipe and press on his eyes and squeeze them shut. After the fifth time he clicked command-C on the video link.

He opened a new box. *I'm sorry,* he wrote. Then he deleted it. Then he wrote it again: *I'm sorry.* Then he deleted it again. *I'm fucking sorry,* he wrote, then deleted that, too.

MR. PINK

Finally he posted the video link, with a tag each for Madeleine Hillary Jasmine Alexis and Jen. *I'm fucking Beretta,* he wrote. 145

Then he closed his computer and sat alone in the dark. ✄

Kate Reed Petty's first novel, True Story, *was published by Viking in 2020. Her fiction has appeared in* Electric Literature *and elsewhere.*

ROBOT

DANIEL MASON

Joyce had been living in Berkeley for six weeks when her sister called and asked if she would like to meet the author.

Her first thought was: But I don't like reading! Penny, however, hadn't given her a chance to answer. The author had just moved in across the street that summer, her sister told her, having accepted a teaching job at Cal. They had met him when he knocked on their door one evening and asked if he might borrow a hammer, and John had gone to help him out. The two had hit it off, she said. Later, when the author's television was waylaid along with most of the rest of his belongings somewhere near Denver, he'd come over to their house to watch the Olympics on TV. "Who would have thought!" said Penny, and added: "But he's just like you and me." Last night they'd watched Nadia Comaneci win her third gold medal. Long ago, the author had traveled in Romania, said Penny, and he told them many things about the country that she hadn't known, about the wine, and Communism, and sheep's cheese. She had always thought that Dracula was from there also, but it turned out that it was a different man, who just went by the same name.

"God I'm so sick of her," said Joyce.

She was sitting in her kitchen, looking through a window onto the balcony of her apartment, where a band of sparrows were batting clumsily about the small red fruit of an unfamiliar Californian plant.

"Who, Nadia?" asked her sister.

Joyce thought: So now you are on a first-name basis? "I just want to be able to turn on the TV without having to look at that smiling little mug," she said.

There was a moment of silence. "Sometimes I don't get you," said Penny. "Who doesn't like Nadia Comaneci?"

"Lots of people," said Joyce.

"Really?" said Penny.

"It's her attitude of superiority," said Joyce. "She thinks she is better than everybody else."

"She *is* better," said Penny.

"In *gymnastics*," said Joyce.

Outside, the gluttony continued unabated. If a cat were to come, the birds wouldn't even notice, thought Joyce. They would deserve it. Over the line she heard her sister take a deep breath, loud, so that Joyce could hear her. "Anyway," said Penny. "About the author."

"Of course," said Joyce.

And her sister described how yesterday evening, after watching—a pause—gymnastics, the author had wandered into the living room and seen a photo of Joyce on the mantel, and asked Penny if it was her sister, and of course Penny had answered, Yes. And then Penny had told him everything: How Joyce, too, had just moved out to California, and how Joyce, too, was a teacher, an elementary school teacher, and how Joyce had been married, but that it was to an asshole and Joyce was divorced now, now lived alone.

"'Bout sums it up," said Joyce.

"He was *really* interested," said Penny. "Said he'd love to meet you. I think he's also unattached."

"Sounds like it," said Joyce.

148   "I hope you don't mind I told him all of that," said Penny. "It is important that people know what they are getting into."

Which is what, in this case? thought Joyce, but she didn't want to start Penny on the subject. Instead, she asked, "Which photo?"

"You know," said Penny. "In the living room. Of Montauk, the beach."

"Montauk," said Joyce, and now remembered. Hoo-wee! "That's an old photo," she said.

Her sister acknowledged this, and added that she had warned the famous author.

Joyce thought, So now this was a "famous" author? "Warned about what, exactly?" she asked.

"Well," said her sister. "He's not exactly a spring chicken either."

"Was that the term *he* used?" asked Joyce.

"Ha!" said Penny. But fair enough: it was her elaboration. Anyway, enough of this, she had to run. She was thinking of a dinner, just the four of them, perhaps on Saturday, not tomorrow, but the next. "It's been what, twelve years?" she asked. "Who knows, the two of you might hit it off."

"Saturday?" said Joyce.

"I don't think you have anything planned," said Penny.

"Let me see," said Joyce. "I'll look here at my calendar." She waited a while, then rustled a few pages near the receiver.

"Sure," she said at last.

"Good," said her sister. And she told Joyce the name of the author. She knew it sounded foreign, she added, but he was completely American, just from New York. "Anyway. In case you want to read one of his books."

"That seems unfair," said Joyce.

"Unfair?" said Penny.

"He hasn't read any of *my* books," said Joyce.

"You haven't written any books," said Penny.

"I mean, in principle," said Joyce.

"Then don't," her sister said. "Then don't."

Actually, it wasn't entirely true she didn't like reading.

Since moving to California, she read the newspaper daily, including the classifieds, and when she left Boston, she'd brought a stack of *Newsweek* she had never gotten around to reading and wanted to finish before renewing her subscription at her new address. In Massachusetts, at the school where she had been a teacher, she liked reading to the children, especially books about characters who weren't actually humans but did human things, had human conundrums, like Sylvester the Donkey, or Frog and Toad. Indeed, sometimes during her class library time, when she was supposed to be cleaning up her classroom, she stayed and listened to the librarian, especially if they were reading one of those. For reasons not apparent to her, she found their challenges and decisions more relatable than those of actual humans. That was on the plus side of reading. On the other side, the minus one, was the feeling that most authors just went on and on, like a conversation with someone who didn't know when it was your turn to talk about yourself. And most of them, to be honest, were hysterics of some sort or another. Such emotion! Such trouble! Most of the problems the characters got themselves into could have been easily avoided by a little caution and modesty. But no one owned up to their mistakes. Back when she was married, Richard had subscribed to Book-of-the-Month Club, the editions of which he read with civic-minded duty. He was always pestering her about them, and so for his sake, she tried. She really did. But she couldn't make it past even the first section—"From the Boundless Deep"—of James Michener's *Hawaii* (December), and Margaret Leech's *In the Days of McKinley* (November) was hardly any easier, even if, as Richard had told her, it was written by a woman. By the time it came to *The Tents of Wickedness*, by Peter De Vries, she'd been so annoyed by the presumptuousness of

150 the epigraph—"We can be nothing without playing at being"—that she'd returned it to the shelf. When at last she ventured the opinion (eloquently, feelingly put, she thought) that none of the writers "spoke to her"—a phrase which, in fact, she'd picked up from reading—Richard had answered that it was not Michener's responsibility to prove himself to Joyce, but Joyce's responsibility to prove herself to Michener. More recently, she'd read part of a smutty romance over the shoulder of her neighbor on the airplane, which, alongside the Fodor's *San Francisco* that she'd purchased before moving, had helped her pass the flight. But so had sleeping, so had Valium. To put it in a nutshell, reading had both pros and cons. What annoyed her more about the phone call was her sister, or perhaps, more precisely, her own dependence on her sister's interference in her life.

It was Penny who had recommended, after Joyce had lost her job at Hillside Elementary in Waltham, that she come west to live near them in Berkeley. The idea had seemed absurd at first. She liked to think she wasn't a square—in '72, she'd been the first person in her neighborhood to have a bumper sticker for McGovern. But from what she knew of Berkeley, her sister might have well told her to go apartment hunting in Gomorrah. A teacher she knew in Waltham had been to San Francisco and seen a couple copulating in the open, even described it with some awe and jealousy. And one of her neighbors had a cousin who'd gone insane from magic mushrooms and eaten his own fingers. Nope: Not for me, she thought. But then the firing happened, and a cold winter followed, and one morning, sitting in her apartment and watching a snow plow struggle against a huge drift which she knew was actually mostly dirt from the excavation of a broken pipeline, it dawned that somehow she had failed. Not just at marriage, she thought, though in the balance, that was certainly not an unreasonable proposition. And not just in her career, for the School Board had been excessive, really, she was sure of that. It was, rather, something bigger, she thought, and it came about that the thing she decided she had failed at was being a person in the world.

Given such circumstances, going to California would have seemed to be nothing short of masochism. For Penny, in the balance, had come to possess all that Joyce did not. Through high school, they had been almost identical. RePenny, Joyce's teachers had called her: the same bright Doris Day smile, the same golden fringe, the figure that earned mention in the yearbook, twice. But Penny, five years ahead, had married John—an assistant football coach—in college, and in the early years they'd moved frequently—Ohio State, Kentucky, Clemson—before settling at Cal. There, Penny raised three sons, now scattered across the country, and while motherhood became her, it seemed to Joyce that this was because it offered her the undisputed opportunity to pursue her true calling, which, Joyce eventually decided, was meddling in other people's lives. Especially if that other person was her only, younger, sister. And so, when Joyce and Richard had finally separated, Penny's joy came less because she didn't like him—she didn't—but more because of the opportunities for interference that this "open field" entailed.

The proximate cause of Richard's departure had been an act of infidelity, which Joyce had discovered one afternoon when her husband, with recklessness that seemed, in retrospect, perhaps not quite so reckless, had called his mistress from their home phone. Penny, as expected, had rallied swiftly to her sister's side; the outrage "actualized" her, thought Joyce, using a word she'd learned from Penny. What Penny didn't know was that the marriage had been moribund almost from the beginning, and for reasons pertaining to the marital bed. The collapse had played out slowly, though the problem, Joyce would realize later, was there from the beginning—the pile of dirt beneath the snowdrift, so to speak: Frozen, unyielding, and messier with each effort at removal. For the heart of the matter, as she came to see it, was that there was something repulsive to her about the senses, all the senses; her mistake had been not to foresee this before it was too late. One might have guessed that a person who was repelled by salad dressing might also be repelled by intercourse. Richard, for his part, considering the damaged goods that he'd been given, was actually rather kind about it, suggesting all variety of accommodation that might assuage his frigid bride. Except it wasn't frigidity. For frigidity implied, at least as Joyce conceived it, an absence of desire. Indeed, her misfortune, she decided, was that desire *hadn't* left her; just any tolerable means by which it could be fulfilled. If only the cure for longing didn't involve the body, she thought, if only the salve for loneliness wasn't other people. But she feared the sympathy that might follow such an admission even more than she feared the prickle of her husband's flesh. For what could she tell him? That she didn't mind if she was held, just not by another person? Who, then, was to do the holding? That sometimes the world seemed too close, too warm, too pressing? That even their marriage counselor wore lipstick that was far too thick, smelled sickly of the cinnamon tea she offered to her clients, used too many phrases like "rekindling passion," which sounded like something burning out of control?

So she told Penny about the infidelity, and was praised for being "brave" to share. And because she'd couldn't admit this other part of her, she'd consented, after the requisite months of what Penny called her "mourning," to go on other dates.

Afterward, Joyce reported dutifully to her sister, detailing each one's failings. The college friend of John's who tried to hold her hand during a movie, fingers still greasy from the popcorn. The brother of a husband of a friend of Penny's who took her—insinuatingly she was certain—out to oysters. The neighbor, who at the end of dinner had offered her a bite of his apple pie, wet with melted ice cream and thus

bearing the appearance of something chewed and then expectorated.
This last one had been a high school drama teacher in her district, who wore black shirts despite his dandruff, was balding already in his late twenties, and in general annoyed her by what seemed to be genuine delight at student performances that were mediocre at best.

"So that's that," she'd told Penny, with some relief. For no one could accuse her of not trying.

"No one else?" her sister had asked her. "What about Walter?"

This was a fourth-grade teacher at Hillside who Joyce once made the mistake of mentioning to Penny.

"A colleague? You must be kidding. Don't drink from the well you piss in, I say," said Joyce.

"I think the saying is 'Don't piss in the well you drink from,'" said Penny.

"But you understand," said Joyce.

"I understand that you are saying a relationship with someone is the same as urinating on your food," said Penny.

They'd agreed to let it drop. She was twenty-six. Instead of daily, they spoke weekly, and when they spoke, they spoke of other things, such as her teaching. For she enjoyed her teaching. Children, she decided, offered a kind of tolerable connection—their demands, though constant, were of a limited emotional range. Distress could be managed by distraction, by candy (though she really wasn't supposed to), by the wiping of a nose followed by a quick washing of the hands. Physically speaking, they weren't ugly in the way most adults were ugly. Aside from a porker or two, their forms were streamlined and efficient, without unnecessary flesh. They asked nothing of her, knew nothing of her, went home with other people when the day was done. They were, she decided, only part human, not unlike Sylvester, Frog, and Toad. Each day, she stayed, late, very late, meticulously cleaning up the mess they made of

154 the classroom, then went home, ate, and—fulfilled, exhausted—slept.

Her dismissal, therefore, had come as a shock, a blow to her very core, to use another phrase she'd probably picked up from reading. The ostensible reason was the complaint of a summer school parent following a class exercise in which she'd had children make cards for family members of crash victims of an Eastern Airlines flight that had been approaching JFK. For years, such letters of consolation had been one of her favorite class activities, and over the course of time, she'd sent packages to the families mourning the victims of coal mine disasters, earthquakes, train wrecks. It had been inspired by an article in *LIFE* about a high school that had sent condolences after a Pennsylvania Railroad train loaded with baseball fans had crashed into the Susquehanna River. There was, she thought, no reason younger students couldn't be taught compassion, and each time she bundled up a package, she liked to imagine the bereaved family opening it to find the multicolored cards and drawings, and being comforted, in their grief, by the kindness and generosity of children.

Unfortunately, this argument had lost against the argument of the complaining parent, and, eventually that of the school board, that first grade was far too early to expose a child to such horrors. As had her follow-up argument, that it allowed them to practice their penmanship and spelling.

She couldn't bear to stay in Waltham after that; her apartment was across the street from the Elementary. Then Penny had told her about a Berkeley summer program in mathematics that had lost half its teenage staff to a mono epidemic. A math camp, in Joyce's hierarchy of pedagogy, sat somewhere around driver's ed. But by then, for the first time in memory, she had taken to suddenly, inexplicable trembling, and so off to the land of drug-fueled outdoor copulation she went, her pile of unread *Newsweek* tucked neatly in her bags.

* * *

When she hung up after her conversation with her sister, Joyce stayed for a moment at the kitchen table. The evening light had shifted slightly; in the window, she could see her own reflection, and for a startling moment, she seemed to be the object of the birds' unrelenting assault. She blinked; they vanished, and she appeared in sharper reflection. She was irritated by her sister for the invitation, and was half of the mind to call her back. But by then she'd begun to learn that solitude is much harder in a new home than an old one, and the possibility of a friendship—and friendship only—seemed not an unreasonable one. No, she thought, reformulating this: it would not be unreasonable at all to have a friend. Indeed she was mildly flattered that the man had noticed her. Yes, some years had passed since the photo had been taken. But unlike Penny, who, in Joyce's opinion, had begun to let herself go—who drank too much, had grown soft about the waist despite her weekly tennis—Joyce maintained a regimen that kept her stomach firm and posture straight.

Reading his books, however, was out of the question. It was not merely the problem of asymmetry; fame she didn't mind. Actually, the way she saw it, or the way she decided that she saw it, fame belonged on a pure plane, while whatever intimacies the man confided in his novels— for they were novels, she assumed—belonged to the same category as dandruff and bites of other people's food. So she was surprised to find, the following afternoon, as she was driving past the branch of the public library on her way to the supermarket, a pinch of curiosity about what she might find inside it. At the very least, she thought, she might see an author photo, and if necessary, call things off. As it turned out, she had some trouble remembering his name exactly, but it was uncommon enough that the librarian recognized it after a couple of tries. In fact, he beamed. The author was one of his favorites, he told her. She'd never

156 read him? Oh, she was in luck!

Hearing this, Joyce felt a surprising pride. She briefly weighed telling the librarian that she was going to be introduced to him, that he'd seen a photo of her in a swimsuit in Montauk, that her sister thought that they would hit it off. But this was probably the kind of thing the librarian heard a lot from crazy people, so she held her tongue.

She, a schoolteacher, could have found the section on her own, but the librarian was so enthusiastic that he had already come out from behind his desk, and it was too awkward to dissuade him. He was a middle-aged man with a beard and a ponytail and a striped, collared short-sleeve cotton shirt tucked behind a belt with some kind of Indian buckle. He must have felt that their shared interest in the author gave him license to go on and on, because he talked officiously as they crossed the library, in the same loud voice that the school librarian used back in Waltham, despite berating the children for the slightest peep. When at last he stopped, she was surprised to find that he had led her to the science fiction section. She hesitated; from her experience at Hillside, she associated science fiction entirely with the fifth- and sixth-grade boys. Before her, a number of the volumes had been displayed to show their covers. Stalwart robots carried limp and helpless humans. Ships like sculpins ventured through the icy crags of towering mountains. Children in spacesuits stared up at distant moons reflected in their helmets. From the top shelf, presumably out of reach of the younger patrons, an array of female life-forms, buxom and reptilian, stared out at the reader with unbridled, trans-cosmic lust. She looked to the librarian, now certain that he'd made an error. Science fiction? Surely, Penny would have mentioned...

"Right here," said the librarian, removing a book from the lowest shelf. And there he was.

One by one he handed them to her. All had library bindings—tan, gray, blue—all, she noted, seemed well-thumbed. When at last he handed her one with a cover wrapped in mylar, she saw a space city hovering above a bright red planet, its keel honeycombed with thousands of portholes. She flipped it over, finding herself staring into the eyes of the man she was to meet. It was so sudden that she froze and looked up, as if the real man would then step out from behind the stacks. It felt like she'd been caught sneaking answers on a test. But the librarian was lost in a table of contents for one of several volumes of short stories, and she reminded herself that the author had already seen a photo of *her,* and in a two-piece swimsuit. She looked again. The photo was from about the same time as the one taken in Montauk; the book was from '59—the year of her wedding—and the author, who wore horn-rimmed glasses and a bow-tie, stared out beneath a thick head of hair that glistened with brilliantine. She was a tad disappointed—he looked more like a chemistry professor than what she had imagined an author would look like, and the photo was a little unflattering with regards to his chin. If he was in his late twenties, he was by now well on his way to being overweight. There was a brief bio beneath the photo, but it told her little more than what her sister had told her, save that he had written some six other books at the time of the printing, and that one of them had won an award she had never heard of. It said that he lived in Brooklyn, or had, back then.

"How many can I check out?" she asked the librarian.

"How many?" he answered, gesturing to take in the bounty of the entire shelf. "This is America, sweetheart. As many as you like."

She took the one with the cover, then three more the librarian recommended. Then she worried she might not find the time or energy to finish them, so she took one of the story collections, just in case. She loaded them into the back of the station wagon she was borrowing from Penny, and drove away. On the radio, there was a news report about

158 Nadia Comaneci, and another, about an earthquake in China, where they expected casualties in the hundreds of thousands, and briefly she felt magnanimously warm, even connected with the nameless multitudes of those less fortunate than she.

At home she carried in the groceries. She was quite hungry all of a sudden, and setting a can of soup to cook, went back out for the books. She was halfway up the stairs when she opened one of the them, out of curiosity, just to read the first paragraph, and day was breaking when she put it down.

For the next week, during every waking hour of the day she wasn't working, Joyce read. Over meals and while she brushed her teeth, at stoplights, during the breaks at school. At night, moving from table to couch to bed and back, she turned the pages slowly, letting the room before her fill with crimson suns and blue-white nebulae. Gilded cities grew up from the carpet, domed outposts on lunar deserts, spinning disks which issued hordes of spindled space-probes. Rockets soared across the heavens, dragging glittering cylinders of ice from Saturn's rings. Cosmic kings called out to her from blazing, floating thrones of iridium and rhodium. She felt people approach, leering space pirates, beautiful women swathed in robes made only of light.

On Mercury, powerful yet docile robots carried their human masters on their strong, broad shoulders, vaulting fissures in the flinty earth with grace.

She went to math camp in the daytime but she didn't really, returned to the library on Thursday, and when Friday came she called in sick.

On Saturday, she spent the morning reading, and when the afternoon came, she got dressed in a short plaid skirt she hadn't worn in years and a cream blouse, which after consideration, she left unbuttoned at the top.

Her sister lived in North Berkeley, across the city and partially up the hill along a winding street. It was a funny-looking house in Joyce's opinion, built back in the 1920s in a style Penny called "fairy-tale Tudor": squat and sprawling, with gabled roofs and a pair of turrets—the architectural equivalent, thought Joyce, of garden gnomes, of which there also were a few. Great oaks rose from its yard, shading the home with massive boughs that would surely take down half the structure in a windstorm. There were ferns and tree ferns, and moss on the brick path that led in from the street. It seemed wildly out of place in sunny California, thought Joyce, torn screaming in pain and terror from its true home in a misty medieval shire. Long ago, Penny had fallen immediately for it, thought it was romantic, and John had been pacified by the basketball hoop and foosball table, which despite the warped wood and squirrels nesting in the goals and the fact that the foosball itself had gone missing sometime during the Johnson administration, he would not throw out.

As usual, the front door was unlocked and Joyce entered without ringing the bell, passed the curving staircase that led upstairs, and followed the long hallway to where it opened into the living room. Beyond was the dining room, and beyond that the kitchen, where she found her sister, aproned, dipping strips of eggplant in a cheesy batter. Their old, useless St. Bernard, half-blind and lame and lazy, lifted its head before going back to sleep. Through a little porthole window in the kitchen wall, Joyce could see John hovering over the grill.

"Apparently you didn't hear about the family in Oakland," said Joyce.

"Hi," said Penny.

"Guy came in, killed the wife and husband, then took his pretty time to rob the place, even ate some cereal while the bodies lay there on the floor."

"Sounds terrible. On the tiles, not the carpet, I hope," said Penny.

"I'm serious," said Joyce.

"I know you are," said Penny. "That might be part of the problem."

She drew another tongue of eggplant through the batter.

"Good to see you too," said Joyce.

Penny winked. She'd had her hair curled; recently, she'd added a tiny bit of russet, which—said Penny—took out the mousy from the blond. Beneath the apron, she wore one of her favorite outfits, a sleeveless green jumpsuit with a winged collar that made her look, in Joyce's opinion, like Robin Hood. I ought to tell her, Joyce thought, but her sister headed off any verbal articulation of this advice by thrusting forth a plate of crudités.

"You know how I feel about ranch dressing," said Joyce.

"I don't," said Penny, "but I can guess."

"No thanks," said Joyce. There were stools at the island, and she sat. She tapped her fingers on the counter.

"You're nervous!" said Penny.

"No. Okay: A little," said Joyce. "Pathetic isn't it?"

"More like human, I'd say," said Penny. There were wine glasses on the counter and she poured Joyce a glass, which Joyce, though she had many opinions about people's irresponsibility with alcohol, gulped quickly. Penny chuckled, refilled it. Almost instantly, Joyce felt her head get light.

"I take it he's not here," said Joyce.

"Not unless he is in the back, murdering John," said Penny. She paused for a moment. "A joke, Joyce. Relax. You came thirty minutes early."

"Did not. You said…"

"Did too," said Penny.

John shouted something from the patio. Penny fished a pan of marinating chicken from the refrigerator. The dog lurched to its feet and stumbled over. "Come, Grizzly," said Penny. "We're summoned."

"Make yourself at home," she said to Joyce.

After a moment's consideration, Joyce filled her glass again, and wandered slowly into the living room, a high-ceilinged, paneled space decorated with a mix of football trophies and large-print family photographs. There was a fireplace, and on the mantel, amidst the team photos and prom shots of her nephews, she saw the photograph at Montauk that had started off this whole to-do. She halted. In the many times she'd been to Penny's, she'd always passed it swiftly, never stopped to look. She didn't mind the photo; what she minded was the other memories, it being from that summer just before their mother's cancer. Before Penny went away to college. Before the live-in nurse took over. Before the night that Joyce, changing her mother's slippery sheets, had seen what the disease had done. A lie, she thought; for she knew the picture showed a joy that wasn't. But now, wondering who it was she had to be that Berkeley evening, she approached and took it down.

In the photo there were six of them, Penny and Joyce and their cousins, standing on a picnic blanket. How young she looked, she thought, though what struck her most was her carefree expression, the apparent obliviousness to a cousin's arm thrown over her shoulder, the hot dog on the checkered blanket before them, the sand that flaked her thighs and feet. Now the thought of such a day, of the heat, the messy jar of mustard, the humid proximity of other bodies seemed incompatible with a look of such freedom and elation. Had there truly been such a change in me? she wondered. Or was it always there, hidden, the true person she was, inside this other person suit.

She looked at her watch, took another sip from her wineglass, and found it empty. Her hand shook a little. The giddiness from the first glasses had already begun to wear off and now she felt a headache coming on. Penny was still outside, so she wandered back down the hallway and upstairs to her sister's bathroom, and after rummaging curiously through

162 her cabinet, found some Tylenol. On the way back out, she passed a bookcase and stopped to look. There was mostly a mix of mysteries and romances and some old schoolbooks, but among the Frederick Forsyth thrillers and Modern Library Classics, between a copy of *Valley of the Dolls* and *The Sensuous Man by "M,"* she found a copy of one of the author's books. It was one she had seen mentioned in the list of "Also by the author" but hadn't read yet—a well-thumbed Lancer paperback with a naked woman on the cover, floating in space with outstretched arms, her breasts wreathed in a stream of stars. Perhaps it was the wine, or perhaps the image of sheer abandon—when one put aside the practical question of how to float in space without asphyxiation—but Joyce felt moved, vaguely aroused even, and she turned to look behind her as if she had been caught looking at *The Sensuous Man*. At home, she had been about halfway through the author's books, when she had become suddenly aware that they were strangely free of sex. This was a relief of course. By then, meeting the man seemed daunting enough, and she had no idea of how she was to talk to him after having read, for example, a worshipful description of some extraterrestrial sexpot, or worse, a penis, alien or not. For she would then spend the evening wondering whether it was *his* penis, or whether interspecies sex with a lizard was the kind of thing that turned him on. But: Nothing. His cosmos was completely chaste. And then, all of a sudden, she was halfway through a collection of stories, when a male and female astronaut found themselves in the hull of a satellite that had been gnawed by space-worms, and she thought, Here it comes. But there was nothing. They didn't even rub their spacesuits together. They fixed the holes caused by the space-worms, which is exactly what she would have done.

Whether the wine, or the excitement of anticipation, she felt different that night, and taking the book, she went and lay down on her sister's bed, kicked off her heels and opened the volume, where a spaceship was being boarded. She was halfway through hyperspace when the doorbell rang.

She found the author standing in the foyer, at the base of the stairs, talking with John. She saw him before he saw her, and it wasn't hard, with some squinting, with some imagination, to recognize him from the photo on the book. He wore the same horn-rimmed glasses, or at least a modern variant. If his hair was thin on top and he now sported a gray-black beard, she recognized the same intelligent expression, the same visionary gaze. The author had brought lilies with him, which Joyce assumed were for her, and was about to descend the last steps and take them, when Penny, hurrying down the long hallway, appeared and with a flourish proclaimed the flowers beautiful—"Really, you shouldn't have!"—and kissed him on the cheek. For a moment, Joyce was taken aback by her sister's manner, which seemed aggressively proprietary, as if she'd forgotten that the purpose of the evening was for Joyce. But then the author turned, and before Joyce knew it, she had descended the last two steps of the staircase. She offered her hand; now he was the one to kiss *her* cheek. Apparently, this was a thing that Californians were into lately, and in general she was against it, but she was pleased at the same time to find he smelled of nothing, none of the cologne that Richard used to apply in quantity, nor that gymnasium odor she had come to associate with men.

"Nice to meet you," said the author.

"Nice to meet you, too," said Joyce.

The dog, claws scratching along the hallway, finally had joined the party. "Grizzly!" proclaimed the author, kneeling in so that the dog licked him sloppily on the mouth.

Thus gathered, the party walked back along the long hallway, single file, and into the living room, where—whether due to the excitement of the moment, or the suspense of the unfinished Lancer paperback,

164 or the fact that the author had just French-kissed an animal that spent half the day licking its genitals, or perhaps simply the week she'd spent on spaceships, in distant galaxies—it was a lot to process, really—Joyce found herself at loss for what to say.

Thankfully Penny was there to save her. "Chardonnay?" she asked the author. "We've already had a couple, right Joyce?"

Speak for yourself! thought Joyce, wondering if she should correct her sister, lest the author think that he'd been set up with a drunk. But then he laughed as if he was relieved to hear this, and she reminded herself that indeed she'd had two, or three, already, and it didn't matter because in a moment they had moved outside, next to the foosball table, and beneath the oak, and there the evening began.

In the beginning, they mostly exchanged pleasantries, and by "they," we mean mostly the author and Penny and John. John inquired as to how the author was getting on with his move and whether his belongings, apparently last spotted somewhere outside Reno, had arrived yet, while Penny asked whether this would be a problem for his classes, to which he replied that he'd been spared teaching that autumn, but—and here he laughed—they better arrive by winter term. Then Penny told a story about how when they had moved to Berkeley from South Carolina, their driver had backed over a pump at a gas station, a story Joyce had never heard before and suspected her sister was inventing. Joyce thought of sharing how she'd taken Valium on the airplane and woken in SFO when a cleaning woman nudged her with a standing dustpan, but decided, in the context of Penny already having presented her as some kind of alcoholic, that this was best kept under wraps. It didn't matter, because the author then asked Penny about the home's previous owners. This was one of Penny's favorite topics, for the man, a widower and a great scholar of either Spanish or Italian literature, had some kind of mental illness that drove him to save all the fat he skimmed from cooking, and for months, she and John uncovered jars of greasy yellow tallow everywhere, leading them to joke that Professor Loomis had boiled down his wife. 165

"Probably he grew up in the Depression," said Joyce.

There was a moment of silence.

"That's why he was saving the cooking fat," said Joyce. "Because of the Depression. Like Grandpa and his strings."

"Yes, Joyce," said Penny. "That's a helpful explanation." There were nods of approbation all around. And the author looked to Joyce and smiled, not in a mocking way, but in a way that seemed to acknowledge that even though she was saying very little, indeed, conversationally speaking, was batting 0 for 1, he was happy she was there.

Again the conversation started up again. Again Joyce didn't know what to say. Or, didn't she? For she had a hundred questions, a thousand questions really—for example, Can you really quarantine an entire solar system? And how do the vidphones transmit across hyperspace? Or—and this from the new book she was reading, how could the people be so trusting of their robot servants given the conditions in which they kept them? And then—on a different topic entirely—and, granted, she knew a book didn't have to describe every detail—when people were in the little space pods for so many hours, days actually, where did they go to the bathroom, did they just empty them into space, or were there regulations? Or, if he didn't mind her getting personal: He didn't have any children of his own, did he? Because there were almost no children in his books.

But no one was giving her a chance to interrupt the conversation, which, by then, had turned to the Olympics, which the author had spent that morning watching in a bar on Shattuck. Track and field, mostly, he elaborated, though he was terribly sorry that gymnastics were over. Indeed, he said, he couldn't get over Nadia Comaneci, and, knowing he had settled upon a topic of universal, international agreement, he turned to Joyce and asked whether she had been amazed as everyone else.

Next to Joyce, Penny took a swift gulp of wine and then another, and then Joyce, after pausing a moment to torment her sister just a little, smiled back at the author and answered, Yes.

"Yes," Joyce added with more force, Nadia, Little Nadia was extraordinary, almost weightless. "It seems as if she floats in space."

For a brief moment, Joyce thought she saw a flicker of something—recognition? admiration?—cross the author's face. "Yes, *weightless*," he said, and then John, who had departed briefly, returned and said the chicken was ready. Would they like to go inside and eat?

Inside, on the great glass table, beneath a chandelier that Penny had blown during her glass-making days, conversation resumed, only now, the author, perhaps recognizing his date's shyness, or perhaps emboldened by Joyce's cosmic Nadia Comaneci comparison, spoke to her directly. He had heard she was a teacher. What level did she teach? he asked her. And then: how had she chosen first grade, and how lovely it must be to pass the day with little people gifted with such imaginations. Joyce felt a bit self-conscious at first, especially with John and Penny watching, but the more the author asked, the more generously she answered. She had never really thought of her job as having anything to do with the imagination. But soon she found herself telling stories of her students' escapades, leaving out the part about how most of the escapades had led to some kind of discipline. She had a great storehouse. She told him about the little girl at Hillside with artist parents who taught the class the word "erotica," and the boy who claimed to have learned hypnosis from a fair and used it to make another child bang his head against the wall. She described the little boy at math camp, visiting from France with academic parents, who had a fancy toy version of the Disney *Love Bug* Herbie. With his accent, it sounded like "herpes," and when the children fought over it, he shouted "I want Herbie! Give me Herbie!" which sounded more like something else.

It occurred to her, about halfway in, that this wasn't exactly what the author was referring to when he extolled children's imaginations, but he laughed anyway, and told equally appalling stories about his students in turn. Why, just before he'd left New York, he had finished grading final papers for a general comp class he was forced to teach in odd years, in which students chose their topics, such as "Milton—the writer and the city" and "Shakespeare—truly great?" and by then Penny had brought out another bottle of Chardonnay.

The author complied—"At least I don't have to drive," he joked—and Joyce also accepted, feeling almost wild—Damn the headache, she'd taken Tylenol. It occurred to her that she had never met somebody so curious about another person as this man was about her. It must have something to do with his being a writer, she thought, and the act of creating characters. Well, this was actually a bit of a puzzle, given that his characters were by far the least compelling parts about his books—totally flat, if she were honest, at least in comparison to the extraordinary plots. But if he could re-imagine entire intergalactic civilizations, what might he do with me? she wondered, and she found that the person she was becoming in his eyes was far more likable than the person who she knew she was. Her head buzzed. Yes, something was happening: Warming, she felt as if she had been welcomed back within the human fold. The answer to the question that she had asked herself before—Would she tell him that she had read his novels and his stories?—now seemed resoundingly in the affirmative, except that the conversation flowed so easily from one topic to the next that she still couldn't find a way to bring it up. It was only when Penny announced that she would get dessert and John offered to help her (Thank you—please—No, both

168 of you stay seated), that Joyce took advantage of the lull, to mention, softly, almost conspiratorially, that she had read "a couple" of his books.

With this, a genuine look of surprise came over his face. "Oh!" exclaimed the author. "So Penny told you! You didn't have to really…" he began, but Joyce interrupted by reaching out and gently touching first the table, and then, very lightly, him. "But I wanted to," she told him, "I loved them." She admitted then to never being a great reader of science fiction (she said nothing of reading generally, but now that attitude belonged to an older self). But his were something different, utterly fantastic. By then Penny and John had returned with a bottle of amaretto and a plate of glistening strawberries, and Joyce could sense that between them there was a kind of silent communication not to interrupt. For the culmination of such a lovely evening was displayed before them, the couple leaning close—her cheeks flushed, his cuffs rolled, her fingers resting on his wrist.

And once she spoke, she held back nothing. She told him how she had started the night after going to the library, and only put the book down when the soup had boiled down and started smoking, that she'd gone back to the library to get check out everything they had. She told him how she couldn't look up at the sky without comparing it to the sky above his planets, that she'd taught herself to look for Mars and Venus, and how, when she gazed at Mercury, she imagined his robots tromping through its glittering magnesium dust. Yes, she said, she had loved his robots, their power, their whimsy, their obedience, the way they carried their human masters through such dangerous worlds. Like parents carrying their children. She spoke of how the civilizations he'd described made her feel both great and small, how she'd felt as if she'd boarded the gleaming rockets with him, how she imagined traveling through the farthest reaches of space.

She had spoken for ten minutes, or perhaps fifteen, her mind humming with the wine and celestial visions, when she became aware

that he seemed to be growing ever more embarrassed, that Penny was watching her with a look she couldn't decipher, that John was staring into his plate. The first thought to occur to her was that she'd been rude in speaking, assuming John and Penny knew the books as well as she did, while the truth was that she had seen only the Lancer paperback on their shelves. And so she apologized, and began to summarize the author's famous trilogy, when, sensing something very wrong, she stopped.

There was a silence. Now a smile spread across the author's face. "Oh! Oh, but this is wonderful," he said. His skin was flushed. For a moment, she thought he might embrace her. He began again. "It's wonderful, but, but… oh I'm so sorry!"

"Oh!" said Joyce.

"I'm not Isaac Asimov," the author said.

Across the table, Joyce sensed Penny shifting slightly, very slightly, in her seat.

"Excuse me?" said Joyce.

"I can see…" said the author. He looked to Penny, who was suddenly absorbed with scooping whipping cream. "Yes," said the author. "If you changed my 'K' for his 'A,' and added an 'R'… and got rid of the 'M'…" And he said his name, which really wasn't very close.

"The 'V' at the end is the same," said John, helpfully.

There was an interstellar silence. By the patio door, Grizzly lurched up from his slumber, growled at some phantasmal visitation, then stirred and curled back into sleep.

"So!" said Penny. Everyone waited, as if their hostess had a plan for their salvation. At last, the author chuckled. "At least you didn't think I was Ursula Le Guin," he said.

Again silence.

"Nevermind," said the author. Then, as if on second thought, he added, "Actually I did love *Left Hand of Darkness.*"

There were some looks around the table. "Ursula—?" said Joyce.

"*Le Guin,*" said the author. "She's local."

And he spelled it, and Joyce acknowledged how it was spelled.

He paused. "Since we are on the topic, I specialize in Donne." He paused again. "Another author."

"And you recently won a big award," added Penny, owning up at last to her role in what had just unfolded. Was continuing to unfold. "And you said one of your books was a *New York Times* Bestseller."

"The Early English Historical Association. Number one for four months."

"*Well,*" said Penny, with a confirmatory tilt to her head.

Joyce folded her napkin into her lap, then folded it again. She felt, she thought, searching for a way to describe what was going on inside her, as Gaal Dronick must have felt on Trantor. The air a little thicker, the gravity a little stronger. Grizzly must have felt it too, for the dog awoke again, sniffed in the direction of the door, and growling, trundled off into the living room.

Together they listened to the fading scratching of his paws.

"I hope I didn't disappoint you, Joyce," said the author.

"Oh, no," she said. Her face really was warm now.

He went on. "I've enjoyed the evening, even if..." He paused, then took a different tact. "You know, I like Asimov too. I've read *Foundation.* And I've been meaning to read the next one in the series. *Second Foundation,* right?"

"*Foundation and Earth,*" said Joyce, quickly.

He seemed not to have heard this. "Hari Seldon!" he said. "I must have been fourteen or fifteen, but I still remember..."

"It's not *Second Foundation,*" repeated Joyce, now with defensiveness.

"*Second Foundation* is the third one in the series. *Foundation and Earth* 171
comes next."

She judged, by Penny's expression, that she had spoken somewhat loudly.

"Duly noted," said the author.

There was a pause. "This is neither here nor there, but I think he's married," the author said.

And then, fortunately, for everyone, there was a knock at the door.

Penny and John exchanged glances. Then Penny's face flushed. "Oh, *shit*," she said, for now her drunk was curdling. "It must be Janet. I promised I would bring her cupcake tins. They are having a party Sunday, tomorrow. *Shit*. And I totally forgot."

She rose, wobbly, and excused herself, clearly relieved to be free of the pall that had settled over everyone. From the kitchen came the banging of pans, a pause and some muttering, then more banging. It was dark outside now, and Joyce could see the room's reflection in the patio windows. No one said anything. The author was swirling his amaretto, pensively. John bizarrely seemed to be humming, very softly to himself. Joyce, now aware of the shredded aftermath of the paper napkin in her lap, reached out and grabbed a strawberry by the green. From the kitchen, more banging, and then at last, a muffled cry of victory, and Penny's footsteps echoed down the hall.

"So," said John, at last, "Will either of you watch the Games tomorrow?"

But no one had time for an answer, for there was a scream and loud clattering. Instantly, all three were on their feet. For a moment, Joyce paused, uncertain of what do with all the napkin shreds, then defiantly brushed them off her lap.

The men were already at the far end of the living room. She followed. Past the fireplace, the Montauk photograph. The hallway was dark,

172 and when she reached the end she found John and the author standing silhouetted in the foyer. Beyond them: Penny, her face ashen, hunching as if she could hide behind her Robin Hood collar, steadying herself on the end of the bannister, beneath the bright glow of the chandelier.

"Joyce?" she said. "Joyce, where are you? They...they...are here for you, Joyce."

It was then Joyce saw the robots, just outside the open door, next to the gnome. Patient as a pair of intergalactic encyclopedia salesmen, looking down upon the humans with red eyes set deep inside their expressionless faces. The light from the foyer reflected on their smooth black pates. Their arms hung at their sides, muscled with pistons and gleaming sheets of metal. For a moment, the two parties stared at each other. Then, ducking their heads, first one robot, and then the other, stepped inside. Penny took two steps backward, reaching for John. The author dropped his glass of amaretto. Grizzly, Joyce realized, had fled.

As the others parted, Joyce stepped forward. Slowly, calmly, her eyes moved from John, to Penny, and at last, the author. No one said anything. That's all? she thought. She felt mildly disappointed in them, in people as a whole. But it didn't matter now.

"I'm Joyce," she said.

Across the foyer, the eyes of the robots flickered in synchrony, in recognition, and a shimmering light passed over the panel of their plated chests. Were they humans, she might have thought that they had shivered. Then, one of them knelt to the floor in the posture of a suitor, hands crossed in its lap. She understood that she was to climb upon its shoulders. For a moment, she hesitated, but only for a moment, for she'd been waiting for a long time, one might say for her entire life. Then she kicked off her heels, and in two strides was at its side. In one hand, she still held the uneaten strawberry. She placed her free hand on its head. There she paused. Her skirt was tight, so tight she had to hike it higher on her thighs before she stepped up on the robot's knee, 173 and threw her leg over its shoulders, and climbed fully on. The robot stood. The metal of its neck was cold against her skin. From deep within it, she felt a purring rising up her tailbone and her spine.

Her face was even with the chandelier now. She was lucky for the stairs, the high ceiling, or she would have struck her head. Below her, the eyes of the people were looking up at her, as if in veneration. She felt a tap on her knee and turned to see the second robot pointing to the strawberry in her fingers.

"You should finish that," it said, in polite, vaguely accented robot English. "You will need both hands where we are going."

"Of course," said Joyce, and took first one bite, and then another, and then handed it the stem. Juice ran over her lips, and she wiped it on the back of her wrist.

Her robot waited as the other passed out through the doorway. Then hers followed, ducking gracefully, as its rider did the same. Before them—above the silent bay, the silent cities—the stars flickered in a moonless sky. A wind whistled through the trees above her, below her, and she leaned in close. ✄

Daniel Mason is the author of the novels The Piano Tuner, A Far Country, *and* The Winter Soldier, *and the story collection* A Registry of My Passage Upon the Earth *(Little, Brown). He is currently an assistant professor of psychiatry at Stanford.*

STEWART BRAND AND SILICON VALLEY'S SOUL

JOHN MARKOFF

In the wake of the 2016 presidential election, the national zeitgeist shifted and Silicon Valley went from being able to do no wrong to being able to do no right. Until then, the Valley had been generally viewed as a magical place, an unending font of technological wonders that were remaking the world at a quickening pace. Then in the space of one election cycle, everything changed. Facebook, which had boldly proclaimed that it was bringing the world together, was shown to be driving it apart. Google, which once tried to set itself apart as a company whose goal was doing no evil, was redefined as an uncaring monopolist. And Twitter became a mouthpiece for a racist and nationalist president.

The transformation was captured in two books that appeared in early 2017. Although they drew significantly different conclusions, both Franklin Foer's *World Without Mind: The Existential Threat of Big Tech* and Jonathan Taplin's *Move Fast and Break Things: How Facebook, Google, and Amazon Cornered Culture and Undermined Democracy* shared a single point of departure. They both began with a biographical sketch of Stewart Brand.

Best known for creating in the fall of 1968 the *Whole Earth Catalog*— the encyclopedic better-living manual which became a bible for the

Baby Boom generation—in the ensuing half-century, Brand has led a remarkably varied career, ranging from journalism to environmental activism. His legend was reinforced in 2020 when historian Jill Lepore congratulated him in her book *If Then: How the Simulmatics Corporation Invented the Future* for coining the term "personal computing," something he introduced in *II Cybernetic Frontiers* (1974), a compact book that reprinted two of Brand's articles from the early 1970s about the then-fashionable world of cybernetics. Lepore takes her narrative about Brand's contribution from one originally constructed by Fred Turner, a Stanford communications scholar, who sketched his interpretation of Brand's role in the construction of our digital culture in *From Counterculture to Cyberculture: Stewart Brand, The Whole Earth and the Rise of Digital Utopianism* (2006).

Turner's argument is that Brand was more than an observer of the emerging Silicon Valley scene. He asserts that Brand brought a libertarian sensibility from his days editing the *Whole Earth Catalog*, which espoused self-reliance over dependence on huge institutions, and transplanted that worldview into a cyberspace commune called the Whole Earth 'Lectronic Link, or the WELL, which he created in 1985. The WELL, in turn, with the aid of an unruly band of Deadheads and Grateful Dead songwriter John Perry Barlow, infected the entire internet with a libertarian culture, dubbed "digital utopianism," that generated the anti-regulatory ethos that was initially expressed in the flowering of the dot-com economy in Silicon Valley in the mid-1990s.

Foer and Taplin, and now Lepore, have extended Turner's original argument to make the case that an unregulated Silicon Valley has brought about the current perilous state of the world, underscored by the role of social media and the internet in promulgating both Brexit and the election of Donald Trump, as well as Trump's more recent efforts to fuel the Capitol mob on January 6. They all make the claim that the

176 Valley's original ideology—or sin, depending on your point of view—can be traced back to Brand and the *Catalog*.

But if anything, there's an argument to be made that Big Tech has lost its way from the optimism found in the opening sentence of the *Catalog*—"We are as Gods and we might as well get good at it."—and from the philosophy made implicit in a question Brand first posed in 1966, during an afternoon acid trip on a San Francisco rooftop: "Why haven't we seen a photograph of the whole earth?" If the Valley has lost its way then Brand's outlook is worth understanding, precisely because his early reframing of the way we look at the world may be the only way out of both the dead end of today's divisive politics and the immediate global threat posed by climate change.

Brand, who in the 1960s described himself as being under the spell of Buckminster Fuller, and who in the *Whole Earth Catalog* propounded the notion that "access to tools" could be transformative, has long been characterized as the Valley's foundational "technological utopian"—the progenitor of the guiding notion woven into every startup's DNA for more than fifty years: that computing technologies will inevitably make the world a better place. The fact that one individual—indeed someone who was not even a technologist and who is thought by many to have been a "hippie prince"—could become so thoroughly identified with high-tech remains extraordinary.

Like Ernest Hemingway, he grew up summering on a wilderness lake in Michigan. He attended Stanford as a member of the Silent Generation of the 1950s then joined the Army for two years. Before journalists and historians—including myself—began to chronicle his life and adventures, Tom Wolfe was the first to write about him, in the opening pages of *The Electric Kool-Aid Acid Test* (1968). Brand was a member of Ken Kesey's Merry Pranksters, and the former Army lieutenant organized the most successful of the Acid Tests—the Trips Festival—the largest of a series of LSD-drenched rock parties that gave birth to the Grateful Dead, the San Francisco music scene, and contributed significantly to the emergence of the '60s counterculture.

Brand, seen here with Neal Cassady and Ken Kesey next to the Merry Prankster bus, was a bridge between the '50s beat era and the '60s counterculture (courtesy Stewart Brand)

Brand's influence has reached far beyond tech. More than twenty books have detailed one aspect or another of his life to make various points about American politics and culture during the second half of the twentieth century.[1]

The literary array can be traced in part to Brand's peripatetic life: he was a moving target. Just as the hippies were arriving in the Haight-Ashbury and creating the counterculture movement, Brand, who had

---

1   In addition to Turner, there is my *What the Dormouse Said: How the Sixties Counterculture Shaped the Personal Computer Industry* (2005), Andrew Kirk's *Counterculture Green: The Whole Earth Catalog and American Environmentalism* (2007), and Sherry L. Smith's *Hippies, Indians, and the Fight for Red Power* (2012), among many others that touch on Brand's influence upon aspects of our culture ranging from environmentalism to technology and consumerism.

178 been drawn to San Francisco by the Beatniks of the '50s, moved down the Peninsula to Menlo Park, pulled there by some irresistible force to see what was happening in the former agriculture center once known as the "Valley of Heart's Delight," and "to let my technology happen here." He had an uncanny knack for being early to the right place, and he had gotten wind that something was afoot on the Peninsula soon after he was discharged in 1962. Setting out to become a photojournalist (or possibly a professional photographer), he was hanging around Stanford on his first assignment when a random visit to the university computer center led him to a darkened room where two young men were playing the first video game, *SpaceWar*, which had been designed by an MIT hacker who had migrated to the West Coast following John McCarthy, the co-founder of the field of artificial intelligence. At that point, the coming of the Silicon era was not on Brand's radar. What had once been the nation's fruit-growing capital had already become an aerospace center, but the region's destiny as the birthplace of the microprocessor and personal computer industry was a few years away. ("Silicon Valley" wouldn't be coined until 1971.) But what he did notice was that the pair were having an "out of body" experience. It was the first inkling of the arrival of what we describe as "cyberspace." At the time, Brand filed away what he saw, only to come back and write about it almost a decade later.

When he did finally describe *SpaceWar* for *Rolling Stone* ("SpaceWar: Fanatic Life and Symbolic Death Among the Computer Bums") at the end of 1972, he would be one of the first to alert the world to the arrival of computer networks, online communities, and personal computers. He opens his article by stating, "Ready or not, computers are coming to the people. That's good news, maybe the best since psychedelics." He was spot on, and he alerted a young generation of Americans—myself included—that something positive was afoot. It was a significant departure from the more skeptical view prevalent then in the counterculture that

computers were the province of big corporations and the military.

Brand, however, did not stick around to watch the power-to-the-people computer world unfold. Soon thereafter, just as the personal computer "revolution" was about to explode in Silicon Valley, he would pick up and move again, this time north to Sausalito where several years later he would create *CoEvolution Quarterly*, an offbeat journal that for the next decade would provide him with a platform to explore cultural, political, and technological trends in America.

There is little question Brand was a technological utopian during the late 1960s when he launched the *Catalog*, but to credit his utopianism with the emergence of the Valley is a misreading of history. His true connection is both more nuanced and, in some ways, misunderstood.

It has been noted he was close to a number of the key researchers who worked for Doug Engelbart, the visionary computer scientist who invented the computer mouse and pioneered (contemporaneously with Ted Nelson) the concept of hypertext, which would become the basis for the World Wide Web. In the fall of 1968, Engelbart gave what technology writer Steven Levy later dubbed "The Mother of All Demos" at the Joint Fall Computer Conference in Menlo Park. Brand ran a video camera at the event, furthering his reputation for being something of a high-IQ Forrest Gump.

The demonstration was indisputably one of the key moments in modern computing history. In a tour-de-force presentation, Engelbart showed roughly a thousand key people in the computing field that the digital future would be interactive. For computer scientists like Alan Kay (who would later pioneer the idea of a "DynaBook," the forerunner of the modern laptop computer), Engelbart's demo was a singular moment that pointed the way toward something that was destined to become a universal knowledge worker's tool.

*Brand famously operated a video camera during Douglas Engelbart's demonstration
of the NLS computing system in the fall of 1968 (courtesy SRI International)*

In 1967, prior to both the Engelbart demonstration and the publication of the first *Catalog*, Brand was trying to organize an educational technology fair to be held at the San Mateo County Fairgrounds. It was a project that had been proposed by his mentor Dick Raymond, an urban economist and business consultant who a year earlier had created the Portola Institute, which was designed originally as an incubator for all kinds of educational ventures and would eventually serve as the breeding ground for the *Catalog* and, some years later, for the Homebrew Computer Club, which gave birth to Apple Computer.

Among the collection of his journals that I read around the time Brand donated them to the Stanford Library in 2000, I found no mention of the Engelbart demonstration, though I had been hoping to find a more detailed account of his role in the event. Apart from being an observer, Brand's role was relatively minor. What I wouldn't discover until years later, when I began researching Brand's biography, was the existence of another journal (not part of the Stanford collection at the time), which he kept as a record of what would be his failed effort to organize the technology fair. (The fair would be stillborn after Brand and his then-wife, Lois Jennings, had a bitter falling out with their partners, a former San Francisco State College student body president and his wife, who were dedicated New Left activists. The rift would leave Brand permanently embittered toward the New Left.) The missing journal, which was eventually given to the Stanford Library in 2018, shows that Brand, who would come to view learning as the key aspect of human experience, was actively trying to recruit Engelbart and his group to participate in the fair, while at the same time Engelbart was trying to draw Brand into *his* orbit.

Back in 1962, Engelbart had begun to articulate the idea that computers would become a universal tool that would augment human progress by both extending the power of the human mind and making it possible for groups of human knowledge workers to make increasingly rapid progress in science and technology. Engelbart had been one of the first to realize that integrated circuit technology would inevitably lead computing power to increase exponentially, and Brand's journal notes how Engelbart described the impact of that technology boost one evening when he and Jennings had him over for dinner. Brand had heard Herman Kahn relate the same idea just a few weeks earlier at an Esalen seminar, and the concept of exponential growth had been codified by Intel co-founder Gordon Moore in 1965, eventually becoming known as "Moore's Law" and achieving the status of a religious belief in Silicon Valley. By the spring of 1968, when he began work on the *Catalog*, Brand was already thoroughly steeped in Engelbart's vision, and it played a significant role in his own thinking about "access to tools," which would become the underlying rationale for his publication. How significant his influence was on Brand has not been fully recognized. (Conversely, too much has been made of the fact that Brand began work on the *Catalog* for his friends who were moving "back to the land."

182 In fact, Brand had decided not to live a rural communal life himself. After briefly dabbling in several communes, he instead decided to put down roots in suburban California, on the edge of Stanford's campus just at the moment Silicon Valley was being formed. Indeed, while it remains linked to the back-to-the-land movement, the *Catalog* would have an impact that far transcended the agrarian turn by part of the counterculture.)

Given early access to the Engelbart NLS computing system, Brand rhapsodized about it in a letter to a friend: "I worked for 2 hours last night online with a fantastically sophisticated interactive computer system and then dreamt most of the night among the tree of choices and clarities." He also brought Ken Kesey to visit Engelbart's lab to see what Brand already understood obviously would be the standard toolset for writers in the future. Kesey walked away from the demonstration shaking his head, remarking that it was the next thing after LSD.

Brand's early proximity to Engelbart makes it necessary to reframe the roots of the *Whole Earth Catalog*. As much as the *Catalog* (which Steve Jobs described as "Google in paperback form, 35 years before Google came along.[2]") would come to symbolize the Valley's technophilia, Brand and his ideas were equally a product of the technology forces already at work on the Peninsula in the late 1960s.

This is not to dispute he had a significant impact on the technology world both as a messenger and as an instigator, but just not in the ways that have been described. The question to pose, then, is whether Brand's "access to tools" philosophy, acquired from Buckminster Fuller and Douglas Engelbart, framed the outlook of Silicon Valley—or was it the other way around? Was Brand an instigator or a messenger? Or a little bit of both?

---

2   2005 Stanford Commencement Address, *https://news.stanford.edu/2005/06/14/jobs-061505/*

Some aspects of Brand's influence were serendipitous. Shutting down the *Catalog* after just three years, in 1971, Brand decided to hold a "Demise Party" to celebrate—but with a surprise twist. The party was held at the recently built San Francisco Exploratorium, and in the midst of the festivities, the emcee announced Brand would give away $20,000 on the condition that all those attending the party could come to a consensus on what the money would be used for. At the end of the evening, after hours of fruitless haggling, the remaining partygoers decided to give the money to Fred Moore, an itinerant draft resister and inveterate community organizer who had come to the microphone several times to say he didn't believe in money, once burning a dollar bill to underscore his opposition to capitalist economics. Ultimately, the money went to Moore in the hope that maybe it did make sense to create resources for, in Moore's words, "information, community, and educational networks." So at dawn, Fred Moore became the steward of the envelope.

Brand just shook his head. It had been an interesting experiment, but he never really expected to see Moore again. *Maybe he'll send a postcard from Mexico,* he thought, as he left the Exploratorium in the morning light.

Instead something magical happened. Building information networks was something that Moore couldn't get out of his mind. He kept contact lists on card files, and he knew enough about computing to realize that a computer would make his networking and organizing more effective. He dreamed of having his own personal computer, and four years later, with another computer hobbyist, he launched the Homebrew Computer Club, which not only spawned Apple but dozens of other companies, jump-starting the personal computer industry. It was not at all the outcome Brand had expected from his experiment, but it was very much in line with the impact of the *Catalog,* which had a similar serendipitous impact on its many readers.

The scope of that impact makes tracking Brand's influence on today's computing world complicated, resulting in overstatement. The narrative popularized by Turner centers on the influence of the WELL. Brand first fantasized about the idea of an online community more than fifteen years earlier. Inspired by Engelbart, immediately after the failure of the education fair, he briefly considered something he described as the Electronic Interconnect Educated Intellect Operation, or E-I-E-I-O, before setting it aside to pursue the venture that would become the *Catalog*.

When he did finally create the WELL (in partnership with Larry Brilliant, a physician who, with a small amount of funding from Steve Jobs, had created a company to develop software to allow people to converse online), it never had more than ten to fifteen thousand users, even in its heyday.[3] Moreover, it was Kevin Kelly, a young Brand protegé, *CoEvolution Quarterly* editor, and WELL board member, who would go on to promulgate the ideas of the WELL when he became the founding editor of *Wired* magazine. Pro-technology and libertarian, Kelly would provide the supposed link that tied the WELL (and with it, Brand) to a set of ideas espoused by *Wired* that were later taken to represent the views of Silicon Valley as a whole: anti-regulation, free market, some even devoted to the "objectivism" of Ayn Rand.

And while Brand has been celebrated for creating the WELL, virtually no one has paid attention to the fact that in 1991 he walked away from his creation, deciding that his effort to build a sustainable online community had been a failure.

---

3   The out-of-scale influence ascribed to the WELL was largely due to a stroke of marketing genius Brand came up with when he created the service: giving free accounts to technology reporters like myself, Steven Levy, and a number of others when it launched. The effect was that we wrote about the WELL, magnifying its importance far beyond its actual numbers.

In 1999 Brand (far left) and Danny Hillis set out to build a mechanical clock designed to run for 10,000 years. Today the clock is almost complete. (courtesy John Markoff)

When he designed that online system, he was already aware of the pitfalls of anonymous online behavior. However, while prohibiting anonymity, the WELL permitted users to adopt multiple screen names and as a result people would attack each other in ways that rarely happened in face-to-face encounters. When the computer service began to have teething problems, Brand—as founder and a member of the board of directors—was criticized unsparingly. Upset that the online service they were paying to use—overloaded by too many simultaneous users—was becoming increasingly difficult to use, irate critics, identified only by their online pseudonyms, savaged Brand.

The attacks were both personal and bitter. One day as he sat at his keyboard he was so upset his hands were trembling. He resigned his position on the WELL board and left for a long vacation in Europe and Africa. Afterward he would tell a *New Yorker* writer that he would never love the WELL again, nor trust its process.

What is most interesting in this case is that although Brand had

186 an early warning of some of the forces that would radically reshape the world three decades later when the cyberworld the WELL presaged became the world's predominant communications channel, he chose to remain publicly optimistic about the societal impact of computer networks. The emergence of an acrimonious and anonymous electronic community that drove Brand away from the WELL foreshadowed on a micro-scale the online culture of trolls, filter bubbles, disinformation, surveillance, and censorship that has come to plague the entire world.

In attempting to draw a conceptual through line from the *Catalog* to the WELL and then the commercial Internet, Brand's actual path is largely ignored. By the time Silicon Valley was gripped with dot-com fervor, for example, Brand was headed in a different direction. In 1999, in collaboration with computer designer Danny Hillis, Brand set out to build a clock that would run for 10,000 years, in effect creating the world's slowest computer. An exercise in what he and Hillis characterize as "long-term thinking," it was a counterpoint to the get-rich-quick mania that had seized the Valley.

Although he has frequently reinvented himself, Brand has been consistent in focusing on human responsibility to the environment. At age seven he would memorize the *Outdoor Life* magazine "Outdoor Life Conservation Pledge": *I give my pledge as an American to save and faithfully to defend from waste the natural resources of my country—its air, soil and minerals, its forests, waters, and wildlife.* Even decades later, after running afoul of the environmental movement he had once helped create,[4] Brand could still recite the Pledge by heart.

This is what sets apart Brand's original environment-centric

---

4   In his 2007 book, *Whole Earth Discipline: An Ecopragmatist Manifesto,* he supported the idea of GMO food and made the argument that battling climate change would require reliance on nuclear power.

technological utopianism from a later Silicon Valley generation of digital libertarians, most clearly represented by PayPal co-founder Peter Thiel, a noted libertarian and, more recently, Trump backer.[5]

So while the Valley's second generation—personal computing—is expressed most clearly in the partnership between Steve Wozniak and Steve Jobs (one simply wanting to share his design with his friends at the Homebrew Computer Club, and the other seeing a vast market for a new technology), the dot-com era's values became increasingly dominated by greed. This cultural shift had nothing to do with *Whole Earth Catalog*.

Indeed, one of the key facts about the integrated circuit technology that rose from the Valley is that each generation of computing technology has touched a larger percentage of humanity. By the 1980s, the microprocessor had led to the personal computer industry, making computers available far beyond the boundaries of both the Valley and the research laboratories that had originally developed computing technologies. And before that, beginning in the 1970s, the rapid emergence of computer networks meant that the technology had already spilled beyond the Valley's borders, bringing political and cultural changes early on. As a result, a national and even global cyberculture informed by libertarian ideals was thriving years before the WELL was created. It was rooted in a wide range of networks and online services that predated the WELL—in some cases by more than a decade—and which were not geographically tied to Silicon Valley. The Source, Compuserve, and even Prodigy were all commercial online services that emerged

---

5   It is something that Jonathan Taplin gets right in *Move Fast and Break Things* when he notes: "By the late 1980s, starting with eventual PayPal founder Peter Thiel's class at Stanford University, the dominant philosophy of Silicon Valley would be based far more heavily on the radical libertarian ideology of Ayn Rand than the commune-based principles of Ken Kesey and Stewart Brand."

188 years before the WELL and had tens or even hundreds of thousands of members. That a digital culture was thriving in the U.S. in the early 1980s is also evident in popular movies such as *WarGames*, a cautionary tale of a teenage computer hacker that celebrated online culture and appeared two years before the WELL was founded.

Moreover, technological utopianism was also thriving and being distributed globally through informal networks such as Usenet, Fidonet, and the ARPAnet, which goes back to the 1960s. (Usenet, which was an informal online discussion system pioneered by two computer science grad students, linked computer research laboratories around the world beginning in 1980. It was significantly influential in spreading "cybercultural" values.) And technological libertarian ideals were flourishing in electronic mailing lists such as HUMAN-NETS, which were widely shared by the ARPAnet and Usenet communities beginning in the 1970s and in 1980.

While the importance of the WELL shouldn't be overstated, a significant and nuanced set of events involving Brand would indeed have a dramatic impact on Silicon Valley. A decade after Brand had originally discovered the world of computer hackers in his 1972 *Rolling Stone* article, Steven Levy returned to the topic of hacker culture in *Hackers: Heroes of the Computer Revolution* (1984). When Kevin Kelly and Brand read the unpublished manuscript, Kelly wondered if the various characters portrayed therein had ever met in person. Brand seized on the idea and with his wife, Ryan Phelan, and Kelly proceeded to organize a small conference bringing together a generation of computer aficionados stretching from the MIT Artificial Intelligence Laboratory to Xerox Palo Alto Research Center and Apple Computer.

A number of computer industry luminaries attended the first Hackers Conference, including Steve Wozniak. At the conference, responding to a point Wozniak was making about the value of sharing information, Brand famously said, "On the one hand information wants 189 to be expensive, because it's so valuable. The right information in the right place just changes your life. On the other hand, information wants to be free, because the cost of getting it out is getting lower and lower all the time." Brand was channeling Gregory Bateson, a longtime mentor who had introduced him to the idea of paradox. This way of thinking had been characteristic of Brand's approach since he was introduced to the concept of coevolution as an undergrad biology student at Stanford.[6]

During the next two decades in Silicon Valley, his brief utterance at the Hackers Conference took on a life of its own, with most who quoted him dropping the first half of his assertion. "Information wants to be free" became the mantra both of the dot-com internet startups, who were busy disrupting the traditional media world, and of the open source software movement that would ultimately remake the computer industry by overthrowing Microsoft's desktop software monopoly. The inherent tension Brand crystallized at the first Hackers Conference has continued to be a flashpoint in the technology world.

Brand's influence is a testament to the complex relationship among technology, culture, and politics. While his path from *Whole Earth Catalog* to modern digital culture is more complex than has been previously described, he clearly has played a significant role at various junctures and events that have shaped the Valley. However, even though he views himself as "conservative," it is inaccurate to lump him in with highly influential digital libertarians such as Peter Thiel, Elon Musk, and Mark Zuckerberg. In *Counterculture Green*, historian Andrew Kirk places Brand within a tradition he describes as "conservative preservationists"—people who are likely to have a

---

6   During the 1960s he had produced two multimedia slide shows, "America Needs Indians" and "WAR:GOD," which both explored different paradoxes in American culture.

 politically conservative outlook or to be apolitical, are not anti-capitalist, and are comfortable with technology. It is a worldview Kirk traces back to Teddy Roosevelt's "wise use" conservationism, and he sees Brand and *Whole Earth* countercultural environmentalism as a reinvigoration of a deep strain of pragmatism in American environmentalism.

That is an accurate account of Brand's early stance. But in a series of interviews I conducted with Brand in 2017, I discovered he has continued to evolve. Although he describes himself as conservative, he is unable to read the *Wall Street Journal* because he finds the editorial page so contemptible. So what kind of a "conservative" is he then?

Some on the Left have categorized Brand according to the 1995 essay "California Ideology," a critique of dot-com neoliberalism made by two British academics. However, in reading *Whole Earth Discipline* it is abundantly clear Brand remains committed to the idea that a powerful and effective government is essential in combating climate change. Rethinking the value of good government came from the year he spent working for Jerry Brown when he was governor of California in the late '70s. His view is hardly an attribute of neoliberalism, and puts him at odds with the Valley's ascendant digital libertarians.

Talking to Brand at length, I came away feeling there is no neat category for him. In many ways, his outlook is more traditionally liberal—support for "free enterprise" but with guardrails to protect worker rights and the environment. Throughout his life he has chosen to view technology as a glass potentially more than half-full, and he continues to argue that a guiding human hand will systematically enhance outcomes, whether they involve terraforming the earth, reducing the impact of climate change, or, as with a campaign he launched in 2011, "reviv[ing] and restor[ing]" species that are increasingly vulnerable to human development.

In a world increasingly defined by divisive political forces, Brand's singular insistence on the value of seeing the whole earth—and by doing so reframe the way humans view their planet so as to instill a new sense of responsibility for it—is more relevant and valuable than ever.[7]

His vision encompasses the best aspirations of Silicon Valley—to become a multicultural home for an eclectic community intent on developing technologies that improve the collective good. Amid the growing backlash against Big Tech, it offers a map for the Valley to find its way back to its roots. More than a half-century after the publication of the *Catalog*, his worldview remains Brand's most significant contribution. It is an approach that remains relevant. ❧

---

7   Briefly in vogue in the 1970s, the notion of a "planetary consciousness" is an idea that his work first provoked in the 1960s.

John Markoff is writing a biography of Stewart Brand that will be published by Penguin Press in 2022. He has reported on Silicon Valley for more than four decades and wrote for many years for the New York Times. *He has written several books about Silicon Valley including* What the Dormouse Said: How the Sixties Counterculture Shaped the Personal Computer Industry *and* Machines of Loving Grace: The Quest for Common Ground between Humans and Robots.

ANTHONY BOURDAIN

WILLIAM BREWER

The more money we come across

the less tarot we do

the more we chew

in silence

staring

at palm trees

glazed red

on wall tiles

the heads of actual palms

lining the drive-thru

masked with smoke

from burning

Paradise

For a week it's lined our lungs

Driving home I strain to see

the exit signs

and toll booth structures

as the radio

debates ways

to stop the kids

from smoking Juuls

between advertisements

for cleaning solutions

I'll use after

the rains have come

to make our rooms smell

like rooms I've never lived in

which are the rooms

I most prefer

Two months now

we've been married

it feels the same

but different

men stopped mentioning

fucking

the same thing forever

and everyone else

started asking

about the future

sometimes just saying the word

for no reason

I'd compliment the Beaujolais

and then

"in the future you should consider

looking into"

over and over

until the word began

to radiate

in my mind

I find myself

spelling it out

letter by letter

on the roof

of my mouth

while up late folding T-shirts

and now it's two

and I'm beside you in bed
envisioning the ripples
on my Celestial
Sleepy Time
Herbal Tea
as I dropped in
my CBD oil
meaning both products
have failed me
once again
and I feel like I
deserve it

For ten years I fell asleep
watching him
wander
Old World cities
and chew
the fattened
parts of animals
but he's been dead since June
now I can't get through
an episode
the future
like a residue
on every frame
how it was there
the whole time
but I failed to see it

We felt like him
we said once
in a foreign country

after a farmer directed us
into a cave
at its end
a secret altar
carved into the limestone
by the once-persecuted
candles burning
in little scooped-out
shelves of rock
a bowl of oil
a vacant space meant
for a holy text

To get there the farmer told us
to walk until we feel like we
should stop then walk
some more and so we did
until the sunglow
of the entrance faded
then disappeared
as we disappeared
in blackness absolute
and stopped
and then you whispered
Can you see me?
No I said
but I know where you are

WILL

WILLIAM BREWER

The living are named for what they're doing.
The dead are named for what they are.
My nickname is an auxiliary verb used to express futurity.
Also: a legal declaration, a wish, probability, mental
powers manifested, the power to control one's action
and emotions. In its full form: the desire to protect,
which I think I'm doing when I say to my wife,
"You don't have to worry about that anymore,"
after she confesses that every time I go into the bathroom
she's afraid I'm going to kill myself—
but I'm not always sure. Before you,
I'm a question; after, I'm command.
When the voice in my head tells me
what to do to myself, there's you between two of me.

William Brewer is the author of I Know Your Kind *(Milkweed Editions), a winner of the National Poetry Series. He is currently a Jones Lecturer at Stanford.*

GENERATIONAL DIFFERENCES

ANTHONY VEASNA SO

1989, Cleveland Elementary, Stockton

By now you've read the story of my life. You asked me to document my memories, and I've written down what you and my grandkids need to know. I was hesitant at first, I won't lie. Why would anyone want to relive *that?* But you were persistent, kept saying, "We can't let your history become lost in time," among other intimations that I'm too decrepit to avoid my own mortality, especially now that your Ba has died. So I relented. For months I culled my memory for gruesome details, the shrapnel of the past you want stowed away for future generations, but mostly for yourself, I suspect. And if you're reading this last section, you're now probably exhausted, defeated from those earlier pages about my time in the camps, my witnessing of all those deaths. My life isn't easy to digest. But forgive me for being your mother, because I am writing this section about you, my only son. Even if you already know the story, I want to explain one more thing, properly. A memory that has gnawed at me for years. This, you should also keep.

I remember with clear eyes, even in my old age, the first time *you* encountered tragedy. It was in August 2000, and we had just moved into our first real home. It would take a lifetime for your Ba and me to pay off the mortgage, but we were still ridiculously grateful, so much so that I was anxious to set up the house, quickly and efficiently, before the school year started. Remaining in that transitory state for too long, I thought, would leave our family forever adrift and uncertain, vulnerable to outside forces.

Naturally, though, unpacking was taking longer than I'd wanted. It was your Ba's fault. He had ordered you—and only you—to sort through the boxes peppering the clean white carpets, all crammed with worthless junk. He needs to learn to work, he told me, when I insisted on doing everything myself. To prepare boys for what the world will give them, that's what your Ba called nuanced parenting; in those days, he wanted desperately to be a good father. Our son is nine years old, I told him, to no effect, and of course, a week later, you hadn't accomplished much of anything. Even when I scolded you to stop dilly-dallying, you bided your time by flipping through the family albums. I believe that was how you came across the photo of Michael Jackson visiting my ESL students.

"Mom, what's in this photo?" you asked, coming up from behind me in the kitchen. I was busy right then, chopping lemongrass and garlic to freeze in the plastic containers that reeked of kroeung, the knife heavy in my overworked hands, the grassy citrus burrowing deep into my nose and piercing my eyes. But you wouldn't stop bothering me for an answer.

"That's Michael Jackson," I said finally, my hands dotted with sticky yellow-green bits. "He's a musician that cared enough to visit us survivors."

Stepping back, you hesitated over your next words. "What do you mean, *survivors?*"

"Nothing," I said, "I don't mean anything by it."

"Tell me what you mean!" you shouted, and kept shouting, your pleas clawing at my eardrums, your thirst for answers growing with each passing second.

I washed my hands and knelt down before you. Heat radiated off your trembling body. "What's wrong, oun?" I asked, placing my hand on your dampened forehead. You felt like a doughy space heater.

"Your hands stink like garlic and soap," you said, pushing my hands away. "That's worse than just garlic."

I smelled my fingers and laughed, because you were right.

"Why are you laughing?" you asked in a flurry. "I know what that word means. I'm not stupid."

"Sometimes I wish you *were*," I responded, rubbing my cold hands together. You were often hot, ready to burst, while my circulation had always been pathetic, as if the blood in my veins had exhausted itself long ago. It was part of our generational difference.

"Well, are you going to *tell* me?" You crossed your arms, straightened your back, which you often did to seem older, closer to the height of the other boys in your class. Something about the look in your eyes felt insurmountable and sad.

"Fine," I said, defeated, thinking about what your Ba would do. "If you really want to know, you can know."

We sat down at the kitchen table. Stacks of dishes and a sewing machine lay between us. I thought about that horrible day—the five kids shot dead, four of them Khmer, all around your age. Then the piercing gunshots and the heartbreaking screams, the chaos of three hundred bodies running in all directions, and then the thirty other kids wounded, decorated with bullet holes, experiencing pain no one should experience, let alone anyone *that* young, and then the blood pooling on the chalked-up concrete, the jungle gym and the monkey bars scarred by a massacre, and then, finally, the man dressed in army-green combat gear, who had shot sixty AK-47 loads into the playground before shooting himself in the head, all to defend his home, his dreams, against the threat of us, a horde of refugees, who had come here because we had no other dreams left. What other choice was there but to escape to this valley of dust and pollen and California smog? Where else could we have gone in the aftermath of genocide? Then I asked myself, How am I supposed to tell you this? Where do I even start?

"Before you were born," I began, trying my hardest to look directly in your eyes. "A very sick man came to Cleveland Elementary...with a gun...and then he shot bullets into the playground." I took a deep breath, studied your face for a reaction, but you didn't give me one. "Some kids died," I continued, "many were injured. This was in 1989, so two years before you were born. That photo you're holding, it was taken because Michael Jackson came to pay his respects to the dead."

I finished speaking and we plunged into silence. I still don't know if it was good parenting to let you know about such events. But I can tell you it was intoxicating, strangely so, to unload a whole chunk of the past onto you, and this intoxication in turn made me feel ashamed, like I had gutted myself in front of my only son.

"What were you doing when it happened?" you finally asked. I could tell that your mind was spinning in circles, that you had a thousand other things to say but couldn't get them out.

"I was alone in my classroom," I said, "watching through the window."

"Mom, that's so *bad!*" you cried, lurching forward and slamming your hands onto the table. "You're never supposed to stand at a window in a shooting! I'm only in the third grade, and even *I* know that."

"*Control* yourself," I said, because I had no further explanation. Of course it was dumb. We lived in a city of gang violence, where campuses went into lockdown whenever a teenage boy dressed in red or blue walked down the street. There was no excuse for not forcing myself to move from the window, the view, to do anything but stand there and watch history bleed out over the playground. All this I knew very well, and I was annoyed to be reminded of that.

The photo was in your hands again, and you were staring at it intently. I remember wondering why exactly, in the first place, you were drawn to this image. Did it catch your eye because it was free of our unsmiling relatives? Was it the Khmer students in the background, the boredom and gloom stuck to their faces, the way their bodies tilted in those half-broken desks? Were you already resentful, as you would be later on in your life, that we'd moved away from the old neighborhood, from all those kids who looked exactly like you?

Or was it Michael Jackson himself? How his skin was simultaneously light and dark and see-through? How his jacket stuck out like a sore thumb in front of kids dressed in hand-me-downs, how it almost glowed, reducing the surrounding students' faces to a dull blue film? You have always been drawn to what couldn't be defined, especially what couldn't be defined by me. And if there was something I couldn't figure out, back then at least, it was Michael Jackson. Come to think of it, though, it was probably just my perm that you noticed in the photo. To this day, I can still feel the curly weight of that unnatural hair.

"Take me to your school," you demanded, and then started rambling. We had to investigate the premises of my classroom, you were saying, to make sure it was safe in case of future attacks. It was clear you had no idea what you'd hunt for once there, but I could also see a stubbornness in your face that would only fester if left unaddressed. I guess that's another part of our generational difference: you believe we deserve answers, that there is always some truth to be uncovered.

"Fine, let's go," I said, getting up to wash the residual garlic off my hands. I figured it was pointless to fight you on this, and I needed to prep my classroom, anyway. Before we left the house, I told you to seal the photo into its album, and then the album into the closet. At least one thing I wanted you to put away.

As I write this section, I can recall many instances when I have been worried about your attitude toward the world, about your acute sense

202 of ... awareness. But driving to Cleveland Elementary that afternoon might have been the first real occurrence of these worries. Other boys, you see, I can't imagine them being so disturbed by their mothers saying *survivors* in passing. A mere slip of the lips was enough to jar your imagination. A single word had sent your thoughts running wild in all directions.

I suppose I am to blame for how upset you got. I don't just mean my clumsy explanation of the photo. I raised you to care deeply, too much so. About words, for one thing. All those years spent working as a bilingual teacher's aide, undoing what Khmer children learned at home, perhaps it had made me paranoid. I thought I needed to ensure your fluency in English, in being American. The last thing I had wanted was for you to end up like your Ba—speaking broken English to angry customers, his life covered in the grease of cars belonging to men who were more American. So I read to you as much as I could, packed your room with dictionaries and encyclopedias, played movies in English constantly in the background, and spoke Khmer only in whispers, behind closed doors. No wonder mere words affected you so much. Even now, you still think language is the key to everything. And that's my fault—I thought the same thing.

Several cars were in the parking lot when we arrived at Cleveland Elementary. It surprised me to see them there, a week before school would start up again. I knew other teachers needed to prep their classrooms, too, but you and I were just on a wholly different mission, and right then, the idea of talking to my coworkers made my face burn.

I turned the engine off and the radio cut into silence. Your light snoring filled the car's interior, along with the one-hundred-degree heat. You had fallen asleep during the thirty-minute drive, exhausted not from your own experiences, I suspect, but from mine. I reached back from the driver's seat and softly stroked your cheek. I didn't want to wake you, not yet.

After a few minutes, you yawned and stretched your arms out wide, as if trying to hold the world in your wingspan, or at least all of Cleveland Elementary. "I had a dream where I found Michael Jackson hiding in your classroom," you said, eyes barely open. "He was up to no good, so I scared him off with my karate moves." For a brief moment, as you punctuated your story with kicks in the air, our day seemed perfectly normal.

I looked at you sternly, pretending to be unamused. "Michael Jackson's a good person for coming to our school. Newspapers took notice of us after that. People gave us donations."

"Yeah, but why didn't he visit sooner, so that people noticed us *before*?" Defiance crept through your voice. "Then no one would've messed with us. We would've been important."

There was an air of truth to the sentiment, even if it sprang from your dream of combat with Michael Jackson; still, I felt the responsibility to say, "Oun, that doesn't make sense."

"Come on!" you cried, now fully awake and unbuckling your seat. "I don't have all day!" So I followed you out of the car and through the parking lot. I allowed you to be our leader.

In my classroom, I sat at my desk, preparing worksheets of mildly useful English words. The stale dust of two months was settling into my lungs. You were on the floor, on your hands and knees, looking under the desks speckled with stale gum, under the crusty old rugs that were never properly vacuumed, which covered sticky floors never properly mopped. Every step in my classroom was a fight to get your shoes unstuck.

Using a system I didn't understand, you tested all the windows, tapping, knocking, and pressing your ears against the glass. After that, you thoroughly examined the cabinets for anything suspicious, opening each one quickly before you hopped back, assumed a fighting stance, and screamed, "Ah *hah!*" Then you thumbed through the books on the shelf, in case there were secret notes stuffed inside the pages, any clues as to the locations of potential dangers. It would've been cute if I hadn't been so exhausted, my classroom a burning furnace, if this whole day hadn't been overtaken by a massacre I had tried to forget. A number of times I wanted to yell at you to be quiet, but I stopped myself. I wanted you to have closure. To forget these ugly feelings.

By the time you were flipping rugs over to examine the hidden patches of tile, I decided you were sufficiently engrossed in your antics to be left alone. And so, gathering a stack of papers I needed to copy and laminate, I told you I would be right back, and then left the room.

The sunlight pounded me in the face as I marched down the hall. I thought about how odd it was for California schools to be made up of detached buildings connected by outdoor halls. The sprawling landscape immediately outside made the school feel *too* integrated with the outer neighborhood, neither a real end to one nor a start to the other, all the borders just blurring together. Walking around, you felt that anything that happened at the school was happening in the streets was happening in people's very front yards. Maybe that was why, even before the shooting, I had never felt like I belonged on the campus.

When my copying was done, I stood outside my classroom and watched you through the windows. You were under the desks now, worming your way through a tight maze of tubular metal legs, your expression creased with lines of concentration. You were lost in your own world, and for a while, I admired your sense of purpose.

Then someone touched my shoulder, startling me from behind. I nearly dropped my copies. "Ravy!" this person exclaimed, and I turned around to see my younger coworker, Ruth, also carrying a bunch of papers. "I'm sorry. I didn't mean to scare you," she said. "How's your summer been?" Her blond hair appeared combative, as if forcing me to register its abundance. A broad smile widened across her face.

"It's been okay," I responded, briskly. After spending two months away from school, I'd forgotten how to interact with someone like this, someone who wore flowery blouses and frilly skirts and had actually chosen, with every door open to her, to be a teacher. I gestured toward the windows. "I'm here with my son."

"How adorable!" She stepped closer and peered through the glass. "What's he *doing*?" she asked, her smile stretching to show more and more teeth.

It may have been her smile that disarmed me, or that I was too absorbed in my own thoughts, but right there, with both of us standing in that haunted playground, the truth spilled out of me, everything that had occurred between me and you. It was one of those moments when—after spending so much time in your own head—you forget that other people take up a different space from your own. Or perhaps I simply needed to confide in someone, anyone, about this unfortunate day.

"Oh, wow," she said, placing her hand on her chest. "That's so awful to have to *deal* with that—and at such a young age...and now he wants to protect you? It's...heartbreaking. Really heartbreaking. I was just a kid then, but still, I remember exactly where I was when the shooting was announced on the news. My mom burst right into tears. You know, I still *think* about all those lost little lives." She looked up at the sky, at heaven, at a cosmic realm that was irrelevant to the parents of those children. No, the universe had already spit their children right back into the world that had destroyed them, reincarnated, reborn to live and die and live again, destined to an eternity of being exhausted, as everything, even the privilege of living, is exhausting when set on repeat. "All those beautiful little souls," she intoned.

Her gaze fixed on me now, and I could tell she wanted a response, like a student waiting for the teacher to identify an answer as right or wrong. It was a demand I received a lot, in fact, being the only Khmer teacher at a school teeming with Khmer youth. My expression was mined for validation a hundred times each day, and all the more so after the shooting.

So we stared at one another—Ruth's eyes searching for a sign of approval, with my own cutting straight into hers—until, from the corner of my sight, your head popped out of the classroom.

"Mom, can we *go* now?" you shouted, half your body still behind the door. "I think I'm ready." My coworker and I broke our gazes and focused our attention on you. The sun hit your face like a spotlight, made your skin look pale while also, somehow, exaggerating its brownness.

"Grab my purse and we can go," I yelled back, grateful for an excuse to end this interaction, to go home, to swap the overheating asphalt for the lingering scent of lemongrass and garlic. I turned toward my coworker, who was now, to my own disbelief, softly crying.

Completely thrown, I found myself taking a step back, even though I knew, logically, that there was nothing outright offensive about her behavior. If anything, she probably had a better heart in her than I did— why else would she be reacting this strongly, years after the shooting had taken place? Yet I felt insulted. I wanted her to stop filtering the world through her own tears. I almost slapped her for crying at the mere sight of you, for conflating you with the memories of dead children. But I only turned away. I felt cold, my hands frozen in the sauna of this late-August day, and, despite myself, as I scanned the playground, I started to laugh.

"How can you—what's so funny?" my coworker said, alarmed.

"It was the morning after Martin Luther King Jr. Day," I answered, not talking to her anymore, really. "We were supposed to teach the 'I Have a Dream' speech."

Then, before she could respond, you jumped through the classroom **207**
doorway and said, "Let's *go!*" as you pointed in the direction of the
parking lot, waving my purse around. My coworker cried harder now,
seeing you act like the genuine, impatient child you were, as she grappled
with my total disregard for her tears. Unable to withstand her presence
any longer, I left her there, without even saying goodbye.

Back in the car, you declared you felt better. We were safe now;
what had happened had already happened, you muttered to yourself, as
if humming a lullaby meant to soothe an infant to sleep, the expression
on your face glazed over, coddled by the heat. Staring out of the car
window, as the liquor stores and strip malls and patches of unused land
whizzed by, you seemed at peace.

My attention began to drift then, as it often did while I drove, and
I remembered how popular Michael Jackson songs had been when your
Ba and I first came to California. They were the only American songs
played at Khmer weddings, in between traditional songs salvaged from
before the regime. "Man in the Mirror" was my favorite, but most Khmer
people, including your Ba, loved "Thriller." Your Ba was so excited when
I told him Michael Jackson would be visiting my very classroom. He
kept reminding me to take photos. He didn't seem to care about anything
else, had told me, the morning after the shooting, *Bad things happen
all the time.* Years later, he would refuse to watch the documentaries
and news specials that accused Michael Jackson of atrocious crimes,
and I would think of that same resigned condolence he had offered me.

I've never really told you about his visit, have I? It was in the
afternoon, a bright winter day, the kind that made you think spring was
around the corner, ready to slap February with blooming flowers and
pollen. My students were reading chapter books in pairs, as neither they
nor I had the energy for an actual lesson, before we heard thunderous
choppers, the deafening drone of an engine, dust and debris swept up

 and into the air. The more shell-shocked students burst into tears. I gathered my class and we headed outside, where the rest of the school awaited our famous visitor. When his helicopter landed on the concrete playground, countless security guards issued from the open doors, like solemn clowns from a tiny car, all of them intimidating in their sunglasses, their black suits imposing an air of restrained brutality. It made me furious to witness all this commotion, all this nonsense, on the very ground those children had died. Their blood was staining the pavement.

Michael Jackson was on campus, from his arrival to his departure, for barely thirty minutes. "Hello, my dear little darlings, I'm so sad to have heard about your tragedy," he said to my kids, in my classroom, and I could not fathom how he had dared to call them *his* darlings. When I asked if he could answer student questions, he only offered, "Let's take a few pictures!"

A week after the visit, I got the photos developed and showed them to your Ba, who marveled at Michael Jackson's luxury brightness for about five minutes. Then, still mad, I threw the photos into the trash. All but the one you found, which I carefully placed into an album. As furious as I was, it felt wrong not to preserve at least one.

But I'm losing track of the story. By the time you learned about the shooting, I'd stopped feeling angry, stopped feeling much of anything, really, until you forced me to explain the whole affair.

"Man in the Mirror" had suddenly come to me as I drove back home from Cleveland Elementary. I found myself humming its tune, the chorus echoing in my head. I even searched through the radio stations, in case the song happened to be playing. Then I glanced at the rearview mirror and saw that you weren't okay at all. You were crying, almost choking from your tears and snot. "Mom!" you shouted in between heavy gasps, "answer me!" I had no idea you were trying to reach me. All the peace you had worked for at my school had fled the car.

One hand on the steering wheel, the other reaching back from the driver's seat, I recklessly tried to console you. I was handing you a bag of pretzels, a bottle of water, anything that might calm you down. The car swerved back and forth as I tried to stop those tears. You sounded like you were continuously reaching for air, a surface to emerge from. Your little spirit was shaken to the core.

"Look, a McDonald's!" I cried, but you were unmoved; still, it felt worth a try. Only after I'd pulled into the drive-through, bought an ice cream cone, and shoved it into your hands did you begin to calm down.

I parked the car behind the McDonald's, next to an abandoned gas station, and we bathed in the stench of used frying oil. From the rearview mirror, I watched your reflection as you devoured the melting mess, opaque white streaks dripping down your hands, the remedy to your crying already going to waste.

"Why were you ignoring me?" you asked, gravely.

"Was I?" I said. "Oh, oun, I'm so sorry—I'm sorry for ignoring you."

"But tell me *why*," you responded. "I was talking to you."

"All I can say is I'm sorry," I offered, as disappointment settled into your face.

You continued licking your ice cream in silence. Taking in your visibly sticky mouth, I thought of Michael Jackson again, the absurdity of his photo jolting our day into being, how the more he had tried to change, to reinvent himself into something completely new, the more he seemed horrifically burdened by what he used to be.

"I'll finish this later," you said, fitting the cone into the cup holder. I was too tired to tell you the ice cream would melt, that only a worthless puddle would be left. It was late, and we needed to get home. We had to finish unpacking.

Even now, so many decades later, I often return to that afternoon of ours, and then I look back on everything else that happened to us,

210 and I think, how silly of me to see our pain as situated in time, confined to the past, contained within it. Don't take this the wrong way, but I should apologize to you, for refusing to be forthcoming into and through your adulthood; before your Ba's death, I was always thrown, perhaps even upset, by your endless curiosity with the regime, the camps, the genocide. Every slight detail you would demand to know, as if understanding that part of my life would explain the entirety of yours. Through my frustration, my clenched teeth, I didn't have the words to say those years were never the sole explanation of anything; that I've always considered the genocide to be the source of all our problems and none of them. Writing this last section about Cleveland Elementary, your first tragedy—maybe that is my way of telling you.

As it happened, as the gunshots were fired, and our kids started crying and bleeding and dying, I stared out of my classroom window and finally understood the brother I never really knew. Why he had committed suicide years before Pol Pot, when no one saw strife on the horizon. How, for my brother, even as a teenager, a child, the weight of life was always too immense to bear.

Then, in a matter of minutes this time, it stopped. We counted the dead, the injured, those left over, and we grieved, as we had for the many lives before and since.

When you think about my history, I don't need you to see everything at once. I don't need you to recall the details of those tragedies that were dropped into my world. Honestly, you don't even have to try. What is nuance in the face of all that we've experienced? But for me, your mother, just remember that, for better or worse, we can be described as survivors. Okay? Know that we've always kept on living. What else could we have done? ✄

....

Anthony Veasna So's writing has been published in The New Yorker, The Paris Review, Granta, *and elsewhere. His story collection,* Afterparties, *will be published in August by Ecco. Born and raised in Stockton, he lived in San Francisco, where he died in 2020.*

REMEMBER THE STRANGERS, THE LIGHTNING, THE WRECKED AFTERNOON

LEAH POOLE OSOWSKI

Withheld, they woke the storm, boarded

the boat and eared the hull to hear

how sound travels through saltwater,

if it too feels buoyant. Who are these us

in this bright green sea? Slaughtering

light, it licks their calves and hooks a strap,

stares down their undertones. Half-naked

they sit on the cushioned benches, absorb

the wake and skiff, the motor a dozen

moans, these barrier islands bearing

witness to what? Their relocation,

their getting-to-know-you town, their first

weekend to an outlying island, crowds

of cordgrass, sawgrass their edges, to where

wouldn't you do? The anchor drifts,

the tide de-escalates, boat beached

and showing white thigh, they walk the path

to hear the sand, ghost crabs bury the daylight.

The storm defrosts, squalls the wail,

arm hair a thousand needle-rush, fresh-cut

postures, dumbstruck girls, pray the day

forgets their faces, prey to wide-open rides,

thunder-fueled and lightning devoted,

how similar—trawling and almost.

Leah Poole Osowski is the author of the poetry collection hover over her *(Kent State University Press).*

Her work has appeared in the Georgia Review, *the* Southern Review, *and elsewhere.*

BONE SAW

ANDREW TONKOVICH

Smuggling in the "nonessential" organs first would be easier, and pose less risk. Their lesser contribution to the ultimate success of our project corresponded, we reckoned, to their presumably less urgent roles in the successful functioning of the human body and our ambitious—if clumsily poetic—effort to combine the studies of anatomy and figurative language. Such was the logic of planning, and staging, this bit of collective alchemy, guerilla theater, political statement, performance art project and rescue. We made it all up as we went along.

If discovered, those very smallest human pieces might arouse less suspicion than early detection of a hip bone, bloody heart, or loudly announcing-itself brain, as in, respectively, the coxal bone (pelvis) so famously connected to (as per the song) the back bone and so on, the heart being so much and always, charmingly, the heart of the matter, the brain suggesting the brains of the operation or, as we named it, more formally, "Operation," after the 1960s mass-produced battery-powered children's entertainment from Hasbro, a recreational if competitive test of hand-eye coordination and fine motor skills with a sense of dark humor.

Inspired, we adopted nicknames for ourselves: "Cavity Sam," "Charley Horse," and "Wish Bone," providing anonymity, animation, appropriation, and assumption, our claim to the potential of imagining.

This solipsistic repurposed empowerment countered the annihilation **213** of same as practiced or stolen by crown princes, ministers, kings, generals, henchmen, and agents through kidnapping, murder, and, famously (infamously) dismemberment. I became "Ezekiel," as the vision-gifted prophet exiled to Babylonia with his god, his creatures and their wheels, his witness, a new doctrine of responsibility, and the role of consoler and comforter. I named our cover band, our *sub rosa* band of irregulars, variously "The Famous Myers Jubilee Singers," "The Delta Rhythm Boys," "Fred Waring and His Pennsylvanians," or "The Four Lads."

And self-exiled we were, in the legendary world capital between the Sea of Marmara and the Black Sea, among minarets, domes, and skyscrapers, where Asia and Europe lock arms in their geography of multiplicity, dichotomy, and possibility: Istanbul, not Constantinople, nobody's business but the Turks.

Finding a lone human body part or fragment would be weird or disturbing, yes, but how much interest or suspicion would it actually engender? Enough to raise the alarm, tell a superior, note in a log? More prudent to shrug and quickly set aside or dispose of the odd item and say nothing. Hard to know considering whatever else went on inside the embassy walls.

Indeed, being confronted with a single feature of human physiology, independent of the whole person, might be misunderstood by those we meant to trick or distract, whether the Scientific Council of Forensics, Royal Guard, butler, administrator, or intelligence official called to examine it by the clerk opening the mail, unwrapping the packages after performing X-ray or other required inspection of parcels.

We'd wait, perhaps days or a week in our hideaway, and try again were they to respond with a change in routine. And then introduce some other of many available organs, systems, skeletal components,

214 proteins—what a piece of work is man!—into the catalog of objects, some pretty weird already, which entered the compound alongside mail: farmers' market vegetables and daily flowers, Chinese takeout, freshly baked flat bread, prescriptions, computer equipment, pool supplies, all variety of botany, geology, and technology required, or at least desired by those inside, emissaries of darkest state power or only its everyday salutations, confirmations, celebrations or mechanisms of officialdom.

Our planning was an impossible exercise in guessing, imagining, in pretending, in vicarious occupation of the animate and inanimate, of projection and mystical speculation, hunches and intimations, and reaching for impossible affinity with strangers, or even enemies. Yet we'd worried for nothing! The pieces, arriving at their puzzle, fell into place. That first group, successfully delivered, included an appendix, with its pleasing, even helpful literary resonance. Also arriving: a small envelope of four wisdom teeth, too clumsily symbolic but similarly instructive, pleasing, or only self-congratulatory. A pair of eyes, windows into the soul, disguised in, respectively, a box of ornate chocolate bon bons and a decorative collection of cheap costume jewelry, garish pieces gift-wrapped. It must be somebody's birthday, we hoped our counterparts would surmise, a gift from a prince or emir or ambassador to his wife or mistress.

The smallest bones also made it in—the delicate malleus, incus, and stapes or, more popularly, "hammer, anvil, and stirrup"—of the middle ear, cleverly (because we valued cleverness, in addition to it of course being demanded) concealed in a box marked earrings. Ten toes and other bones of the feet, phalanx, tarsals, metatarsals, inserted into various hand-held percussion instruments, to rattle around. The pineal gland. Two ears. A tongue. The entire operation was supervised by a team of medical professionals, with input from forensic examiners, black market merchants, and an ethics advisor, and lots of dry ice.

The deliveries were caught on tape, recorded, "footage" it is called, serving up more inference, echo, and, indeed, hopefulness by way of the contents: ankle bones packaged in sneakers, talus and tarsals and metatarsals in socks and boots, in boxes labeled *Blahnik* and *Louboutin* and *Saint Laurent*. Sample descriptive language: "Yeti feather-trimmed suede over-the-knee boots," which could mean anything.

We waited hours, then a day. We assessed the video record and reviewed our surveillance via eyewitnesses, photographs, a drone. Such corroboration felt as if we were living, or remembering, a long-ago forgotten story. Once upon a time. In the beginning. Or only making it up, perhaps convincingly. The old tale or fable was as available, as observable as we made it, insofar as what happened inside the palatial offices and residence, headquarters of the Consul-General blocks from the strait, could be made sense of through the denials, phony investigation, scapegoating of obvious patsies and comic obfuscation by the cartoon President.

We monitored each arrival of postal carriers, overnight couriers, government envoys, messengers, UPS, FedEx, OnTrac, GSO, DHL, items sent from across town or the nearby airport, shipped ground, overnight, or priority mail. There was tracking and delivery confirmation via email, text messaging, rerouted telephone numbers, the enhance function on our own cameras, each machine confirming the acceptance by security staff, housekeeping, or official concierge employed by his or her proud nation to stand at the front door of the Embassy and be persuaded, fooled.

We watched for reaction from the consulate: invasion, deportation, press conference, firing, deployment, or cancellation of travel? None. Only the everyday achievement of wealth and the ongoing oppression, for years, of a small neighboring country, the subordination of women, the derricks aflame, the men in their god-robes and luxury automobiles. There seemed to be no entry by unaccounted-for personnel, no suspicious visitors, no obvious intelligence types coming or going in their oversized sunglasses and baseball caps, no servants or bodyguards departing with suitcases or packages, no arrival by, say, uniformed plumbers or handymen or delivery men rolling in vats of what might be chemicals, no men in overcoats carrying packages shaped liked medical instruments.

Encouraged, affirmed, we next delivered the middle-sized organs—spleen, stomach, reproductive organs (in this case male), colon and kidneys and gall bladder—arranged and packaged to resemble dried fruit or sculpture or foodstuffs (preserves, jarred and bottled in oil, wrapped in oil cloth) and shrink-wrapped.

And, then, on the final morning, the biggest bones—femur, tibia, fibula, cranium, humerus, ulna, ribs, sternum, and innominate bone (otherwise called the hip)—big, indeed, and each calling for especial accommodation, in a golf bag, wrapped in curtain rods, arriving in Styrofoam, in a crate, "This side up" or "Fragile" or "Contents Under Pressure."

❄　❄　❄

Nota bene: There are two-hundred and six bones in the adult human body. Only a few are thick, solid, and sturdy enough to require the application of a bone saw, hacksaw, sabre saw, or costotome, of a sternal saw or reciprocating bone cutter. Or the reliable and ever-true Gigli saw, more on which beyond its name would be too much explanation, more history and context than any body, anybody, could stand.

There are seventy-nine organs in the human body, or so we determined, decided, agreed on, risking duplication when we could not in fact establish the definition of an organ, more interested in how these worked together than apart. Our protest was an experiment, on top of everything else. You might wonder: Can you have too many bones, organs? No, not in our endeavor. Too much heart? A brain separate from a body, a consciousness? Teeth are bones, we decided. A ligament is a membrane. A duodenum is not even up for discussion. For our purposes salivary glands did not make much difference one way or another. On the other hand, so to speak, why not? And what is a fingernail, finally? Who says? What *are* lips, hair, tonsils? Adding all these up brought us to four hundred deliveries, spread over four days. It had taken three months to plan, Christmas around the corner. It was a busy, magical, celebratory season of abundance.

✳ ✳ ✳

The power of technology (Greek: "systematic treatment"), we are promised, we are asked to believe, we are given to or coerced into accepting, or exchanging or trading up to or earning points toward or going large with or replacing for our own imaginations, is *our* power, and so why not acknowledge it, right here, right now? It was the season for just this kind of miracle. Why not claim the techno-mystical, for ourselves, for good? We relied on a device, a vehicle, so extraordinarily perfect and right for The Operation that you would have thought somebody had invented it, made it up for this express purpose. Someone did! We did. A small two-door automobile, it was outfitted to resemble a Google Maps GPS-bearing cartographic photo-generating car ("Street View"), but in fact it carried a chromosome-targeting super-ray broadcaster, the blast of its electro-genetic stimulator surreptitiously reaching through the concrete, wood, and glass of the magnificent consular residence at Akasyalı Sk. Number 6, 34330 in the Beşiktaş district, and gently shocking each and every one of those four hundred human puzzle pieces.

And so they were triggered, brought to life, awakening first their cellular self-perception, then awareness of themselves in the bigger world. Then, to their purpose and responsibilities to others, to one another, to exiles and the lost and displaced, and to their purposefully

218 constructed if still unlikely circumstances, their civic roles. Invited or commanded or fated to immediately and urgently embrace their impulse to mature, to engage, to act—physiologically, as only an organ or bone or tissue or membrane can!—to respond, biologically, both individually and collectively.

Here, assembled, reassembled, was the history of a species, of its development and reproduction, with its built-in directive to be all of what only it could be, to achieve its role, its place in only the way it can and must, as something bigger, whole, restored. *Dem bones, dem bones gonna walk around. Now hear the word of the Lord.*

*   *   *

The Operation's success would not, could not be contained, captured, or constrained. As we'd planned, each organ quickly grew its own host. In minutes, the toe bone connected itself to the foot bone. Foot bone connected to the heel bone. *Heel bone connected to the ankle bone to the shin bone to the knee bone to the thigh bone hip bone back bone shoulder bone neck bone.* With veins, arteries, skin, hair, even stink and sweat.

And with each fully formed, fully functioning, new, naked, complete human person emerging from the consul, all four hundred of them, the necessary consequence of the sudden overflow inside the quarters, this neonatal group assembly, our work was realized, and our judgment, our creation, revealed.

We placed the press calls, posted the images, and quickly abandoned our secret location, surrendering our beautiful monsters to their circumstance, taking with us only our magical vehicle and quickly making our respective getaways to waiting vans, buses, motor scooters, water taxis idling on the Bosphorus. Our work was done. These newborns, identical in every way—each a naked, pudgy, gray-bearded, balding, nearly sixty-year-old man—would be clothed, fed, welcomed,

interrogated, exclaimed over, and protected by conscience, science, art, **219**
and international law, if likely also taken into custody for study, hidden
away for their own protection. They would provide no answers, finally,
or explanations, and offer only one name, the same name, four hundred
times, the word made flesh.

Dem bones, dem bones gonna walk around!

Here revealed was a human verity, undeniable, unbelievable,
organized for all who could see, those who might hear, touch, apprehend,
and know: a parade marching single-file right out of the wide-open
double-doorway, exposed in daylight on the street outside the Embassy,
to be welcomed by reporters, witnesses, live-streamers, with at once
nowhere and everywhere to go, perhaps on to the next valley of dry
bones, where today and always wait, impatiently, so many more.

Where to navigate the vehicle next? Perhaps we'd meet again on
the island beach where lay the child's limp body. To the cages where
the refugees were detained. To the river, with migrants drowned in
it, or to rescue and revive the bodies discovered in the desert. To the
kidnapped and buried students, the citizens trapped in their own ancient
bombed-out cities, perhaps to the headquarters, capitals, or seats of
power where reside the killers. ✄

Andrew Tonkovich is the editor of Santa Monica Review *and is the author of two collections,* The Diary
of Anne Frank *and* Keeping Tahoe Blue. *His writing has been published in* The Rattling Wall, *the* Los
Angeles Review of Books *and* Best American Nonrequired Reading.

COMMUNITY SUPPORT
FOR LITERATURE & THE ARTS

The Booksmith

City Lights Bookstore

Community of Writers

Green Apple Books & Music

Humboldt Distillery

Modernism

Skylight Books

Stanford Continuing Studies

ADDITIONAL SUPPORT PROVIDED BY